Leading Kingdom Influencers' Endorsements on *55 Power Points to Building, Balancing, and Birthing Your Prophetic Gift*

It isn't often that God chooses someone who truly speaks with clarity concerning operating in the prophetic. Revelation can become contaminated when gifted seers are not grounded in the Word. Prophet Deland John Coleman is one of God's chosen servants who has captured in his telephoto lens a new clarity for a new generation of prophets. This unusual scriptural foundation of pursuit brings new light to an office that is so necessary to the Body of Christ. This book is a part of God's order for a rising new prophetic generation.

> **~ Bishop Charles Martin, All Nations Champion Church, Oklahoma City, OK**

This is a book packed with powerful keys that will help you in your divine destiny! You will discern how to hear God's voice, how to see in the Spirit, and how to discern a prophet among you. My friend, Prophet John Coleman, is a unique voice who has a heart for God and a heart to see the Body of Christ making a significant impact in the world!

> **~ Prophet Jesse Shamp, Kingdom Culture International, Nashville, TN**

After reading your new book, *55 Power Points to Building, Balancing, and Birthing Your Prophetic Gift*, I was so very blessed. I see and also understand the purpose of the book, which is to build a strong foundation and to make sure that those who are operating in the prophetic are balanced, schooled, and matured, so that we can receive the double portion. Each of the fifty-five points are accurate, full of word and substance, and are coming from a seasoned prophet in the kingdom, with a deep well of revelation and understanding.

You have done a great job. I am very inspired. I am definitely going to use this book in my prophetic schools and will surely recommend it to my students.

Looking forward to connecting with you more on a deeper level.

~ **Apostle Alexander Stekelenburg, Eagles Nest International, Utrecht, Netherlands**

I believe that this book will help those who have been called to walk in the office of the prophet and who are watching the pitfalls of this next generation already to begin to unfold. This book will help bring back integrity and character and will serve as a tool for those who walk in the prophetic and what I like to call *prophetic balance*. This is the book that I will keep in my personal library as a teaching tool.

~ **Bishop Stanley Williams, The Church 3:20, Jacksonville, FL**

Prophet D. John Coleman's book..."Wow!" was all I could say once I had finished reading it. I was left with an overwhelming conviction for personal accountability at even greater levels of stewardship for the gift of God on my own life. Many concepts have been taught by others; however, this is the most orderly and concise handbook for the prophetic that I have ever read.

If someone has a call on their life or is seeking to mature in their gift... this book will bring tears as the love of God overflows in the pages of instruction. The Scriptures are beautifully tied together to make the prophetic "make sense," to bring an understanding of why character is still important today, and to bring change to previous erroneous conclusions otherwise named as "mindsets." So many times, I've read books that seemed good but only focused on one particular area and ignored other things of importance. Prophet D. John Coleman's book is a concise, welcome addition to anyone's kingdom toolbox! Many Blessings!

~ **Prophet Tiffany Blackwell, Emergence University/ Tiffany Blackwell Ministries, Founder, Prophetic Pools Prayer House, Apostle, Shreveport, LA**

Get ready to receive revelation that will fine-tune your prophetic ear. Written within the pages of this book are points and strategies to birth, preserve, and increase the prophetic in your life. Through his years of experience, Prophet Coleman is able to impart insight that will help you accelerate in your prophetic gift. Whether you are just beginning your journey or are already a seasoned prophet, this book will help you to further mature your gift.

~ **Prophet Andrew Towe, Lead Pastor,
Ramp Church, Chattanooga, TN**

"Prophetic Diversity is developed through fellowship with the Holy Spirit, not public personalities! You don't need to be a carbon copy of an original, be authentic and be the best you!" - *Prophet Deland John Coleman*

Prophet Coleman has given an in-depth understanding and teaching, as well as instruction from his many years of walking in the "Office of a Prophet" that will assist those seeking God for clarity in building, remaining balanced, and birthing the prophetic in their own lives.

Founded on Scripture, Prophet Coleman helps the reader to understand that although there are "prophetic diversities" in the Kingdom of God, we must adhere and remain in a foundational stance of solidarity, especially when it comes to the "Office of the Prophet." Thank you, Prophet of God, for such "truth in action," given with a down-to-earth teaching and biblical exposition in the "Principles of the Prophetic," as we remain authentic in birthing, building, and remaining balanced, concerning the assignment Father God has placed upon our lives.

~ **Dr. Brett Watson, Emerge Life Church, Brett Watson Ministries, Apostle / Pastor / CEO / Int'l. Crusade Speaker, Fort Lauderdale, FL**

The *55 Power Points to Building, Balancing, and Birthing your Prophetic Gift* is a much-needed guide and encouragement for the Body of Christ, especially to those who recognize their prophetic gifting in their life. There will never be a time in our lives in which we achieve all knowledge, understanding, and wisdom. We will always be learning, growing, and adapting for the advancement of the Kingdom of God. This book will help the individual who has a desire to grow and expand their ability to impact their local church, community, and region. I am grateful for those who take the time to encourage and equip others with their prophetic development, as Deland John Coleman has done with this book. I believe that you, the reader, will be challenged and reminded of your greater purpose in this life to help others for the glory of the Lord. Take advantage of it today and go advance the Kingdom of God!

~ **Prophet Ryan Johnson, Founder, Ryan Johnson Ministries, Panama City, FL**

Finding prophetic voices anchored in the Word of God and under the influence of the Holy Spirit is very rare in our culture and age of information. I'm honored to know John Coleman the Prophet as such. The love of the Father leaks off the pages of this book and calls and encourages generation after generation to remove the practices that harm us and thrust us into a relationship with the Holy Spirit, to see an awakening of healthy and whole prophets and prophetic gifts.

~ **Pastor Kris Dillard, Marked Church, Executive Pastor, Markt Music, CEO, Fayetteville, NC**

We live in an age with much *talk* of the prophetic and little *experience, wisdom,* and *knowledge of the Word* concerning it. In this book, Dr. Coleman clearly, concisely, and confidently creates a framework for an effective, weighty, and long-lasting prophetic ministry that will stand the test of time. As you read, let these Power Points act as mile markers and boundary stones on your journey with the Lord into the fullness of your prophetic destiny. You will be challenged, you will be strengthened, and you will grow in your expression of purity in the prophetic.

~ **Prophet Justin Allen, Global Awakening Associate, Perpetual Springs Ministries, Founder, Knoxville, TN**

55 Power Points to BUILDING, BALANCING, and Birthing Your Prophetic Gift

D. John Coleman

DELAND JOHN COLEMAN
MINISTRIES

In Conjunction with

55 Power Points to Building, Balancing, and Birthing Your Prophetic Gift
by D. John Coleman

All Scriptures used are from the **KJV, AMP, NKJV,** and **NIV** unless otherwise noted.

The Holy Bible, New International Version® (**NIV**)® Copyright © 1973, 1978, 1984, 2011 by Biblica, Inc.® Used by permission. All rights reserved worldwide.

New King James Version® **NKJV** Copyright © 1982 by Thomas Nelson. Used by permission. All rights reserved.

Amplified Bible **(AMP)** Copyright © 2015 by The Lockman Foundation, La Habra, CA 90631. All rights reserved.

King James Version **(KJV)**: Public Domain

Sites of references and resources:
- Bibleinfo.com
- Biblestudytools.com (Public Domain)
- Blueletterbible.org
- Biblegateway.com
- Dictionary.com
- Wikipedia.org
- Merriam-Webster.com
- Google.com
- Christianquotes.info
- Bibletools.org
- Knowing-Jesus.com
- Kingjamesbibleonline.org

Cover design, editing, book layout, and publishing services by KishKnows, Inc., Richton Park, Illinois, 708-252-DOIT

admin@kishknows.com, www.kishknows.com

ISBN 978-1-7325756-2-2
LCCN 2019921042

All rights reserved. No part of this book may be reproduced, distributed, or transmitted in any form or by any means, including photocopying, recording, digital scanning, or other electronic or mechanical methods, without the prior written permission of the publisher, except in the case of brief quotations embodied in critical reviews and certain other non-commercial uses permitted by copyright law. For permission requests, please contact D. John Coleman.

Copyright © 2019 by D. John Coleman.

Printed in the United States of America

Dedication

I am eternally grateful for all the Thoroughbreds who have been supportive and consistent on this journey with me in the prophetic.

Thanks to all of the prayer partners and those of you who have partnered with me throughout these last few years.

I want to thank God for those of you who have personally sowed into my life.

To all of my close family and friends, thank you for your love and support.

To my family, who have once again given me the space and time to pen this "blueprint of my heart" as it relates to the prophetic ministry.

To my wife, Kisia L. Coleman, and our daughter, Kennedy, who have supported me in more ways than I could have ever imagined. To my other children: my son, Christian, two nieces, Ca'Koia and Rain, and nephew, Jream, I love you all dearly…"to the moon and back!"

Contents

Foreword xiii
Introduction xv
Prophecy xxiii
1. Prophetic Diversity 1
2. Beware of Deception in the Prophetic Ministry 3
3. Three Major Essentials to the Prophetic Ministry 7
4. Prophets! You Must Know His Voice 11
5. Allow Him to Dress Your Prophetic Gift 13
6. Prayer Ignites the Prophetic 15
7. The Elijah-Elisha Exchange 17
8. Serving a Prophetic Anointing Can Increase Yours 19
9. Don't Disconnect from Divine Appointments 23
10. The Prophetic Is Not an Excuse to Be in Error 31
11. Prophecy Is Not Based on a Hunch 35
12. A Prophet's Journey in the Word 37
13. Prophets Develop Their Gift in the Dark Room 39
14. Requirements for the Prophetic 41
15. Don't Dilute the Truth of the Prophetic 43
16. Plant Your Gift so Your Roots Can Grow 47
17. Prophetic Objectives 49
18. Listening and Learning Lead to Longevity 53
19. Strange Fire 57
20. The Prophetic Connects Your Heart and Mind to Purpose 59
21. Design of the Prophetic Gift 61
22. The Prophetic Balance 63

23. Motivation and Manipulation 65
24. The Environment of the Prophet 67
25. Strong Traits of a Prophet 69
26. DOD: Discernment, Order, and Discipline 73
27. Public and Private Interpretations 75
28. Prophetic Words Are Not Always Final 83
29. Keys to Successful Prophetic Ministry 87
30. Prophetic Gifts Type 91
31. Self-made Prophets 93
32. The Importance of Foundation 95
33. Thriving on the Wrong Things Can Be Dangerous 103
34. The Prophet, the Logos, and the Rhema Word 105
35. No Freelancing in the Prophetic 109
36. Truth Will Hold You Accountable if You Let It 111
37. The Danger of Divination 115
38. Truth or Error, It's Your Choice 117
39. Self-Gratification vs. Service-Edification 119
40. The Nature of the Prophetic Is Clarity Not Confusion 123
41. Beware of False Prophets 125
42. Prophets Unpack Destinies 133
43. Signs Don't Always Validate Authenticity 137
44. The Prophet's Nature 141
45. The Prophet's Spiritual Diet 143
46. The Prophet's Home Is Not the Platform, but His Presence 151
47. The Watchman Prophet 153
48. Prophets Increase as They Stay Under the Mantle 155
49. Disconnecting from Self 161
50. Prophets Are Not Here to Accommodate 163
51. Diligence Is Required in the Prophetic Ministry 165
52. Prophetic Print 173
53. The Core of the Prophetic Ministry 177
54. Filtering Your Prophetic Gift Through Love 179
55. Continue to Present Your Bodies as a Sacrifice 189

Appendix

Prophetic Decrees and Declarations 195
A Short Summary of the Prophets in the Bible and Their
    Significance...197
Scriptures on Prophesying in the Amplified Bible.......................203
Scriptures on the Three Things Jesus Emphasized to His
    Disciples That Will Increase Your Prophetic Gift.................209
Scriptures on Gifts and How to Use Them 219
Prayer for Prophetic Ministry Gifts..223
Prophecy 225
Recommended Resources for Reading 229
Author Biography..231
Author Contact Information 233

Foreword

In Dr. Deland's newest book, *55 Power Points to Building, Balancing, and Birthing Your Prophetic Gift*, we find many answers to probing questions so many have in their gifting from our Abba Father.

The reason so many kingdom people lack knowledge in their gifts is because there was no vision to follow in previous generations. This book reveals the vision of God's Word structured for the understanding needed for such a time as this. As the **Book of Proverbs 29:18** expresses:

"Where there is no vision, the people perish: but he that keepeth the law, happy is he."

This book you are reading is a compiled collection of how to flow in the office of a prophet, that could be a comparison to the school of the prophets. It's a college course of wisdom, knowledge, and understanding that would have made Elijah zealous to read.

If this is you, get ready for the most revealing prophetic season of all seasons. Remember…the prophets *longed* for these days. They knew that these times we are privileged to live in will usher in the anticipated arrival of Jesus Christ, and we will all become "One New Man" because Jesus is the Spirit of prophecy!

Sit back, take notes, and mark those items that arrest your spirit. Keep this book handy for the days ahead. Those called into the Army of the Prophets will need the Holy Bible and this book to guide them into the unveiling mysteries awaiting us!

~ **Drs. Frank and Karen Sumrall,**
Sumrall Global Ministries, Bristol, VA

Introduction

1 Corinthians 14:39 (AMP)

> *"Therefore, believers, desire earnestly to prophesy [to foretell the future, to speak a new message from God to the people], and do not forbid speaking in unknown tongues."*

I want to take this opportunity to explain the significance of the number "55." I strongly sense by the Spirit of God that we are going to see a greater depth and dimension of the prophetic in this hour. The anointing of the double, I believe, will rest on your prophetic gift!

The number five represents the number of graces. So, when there are two of the fives together, the implication here is the *double*—double grace on your life and your gifts.

When you search the Scriptures, you'll see that there were several instances with the term, where a double portion or double amount was implied. Some examples follow:

1 Samuel 1:5 (NIV)

> *"But to Hannah he gave a **double portion** because he loved her, and the Lord had closed her womb."*

2 Kings 2:9 (NIV)

> *"When they had crossed, Elijah said to Elisha, 'Tell me, what can I do for you before I am taken from you?' 'Let me inherit a **double portion** of your spirit,' Elisha replied."*

Isaiah 61:7 (NIV)

*"Instead of your shame you will receive a **double portion**, and instead of disgrace you will rejoice in your inheritance. And so, you will inherit a **double portion** in your land, and everlasting joy will be yours."*

Revelation 18:6 (NIV)

*"Give back to her as she has given; pay her back **double** for what she has done. Pour her a **double portion** from her own cup."*

I believe that as a prophetic culture, there is a need for a double portion of the prophetic anointing; however, it *must* be appropriated with wisdom. This is why we need the apostolic fathers, mothers, teachers, and mentors to rise up, with minimal insecurities operating in their lives and abundant confidence in who they are. We need people who are willing to pour back into those who are up-and-coming.

Now, when it comes to your prophetic gift, it won't just happen automatically. It will require *a personal investment* in your prophetic assignment. For example, whatever your profession might be, whether it's secular or spiritual, you are required to have a special skillset. This will help you to accomplish the objectives that may be presented to you.

Our visual generation gravitates toward hands-on activities. We seek to get involved with the task-at-hand immediately, because we believe that will do the most for us.

Examples would be taking a class, attending seminary, or teaching at or participating in a seminar that relates to your area of gifting.

There are so many options at our disposal. You can acquire knowledge via social media, (Facebook, YouTube, Instagram) video conferencing, and so many other avenues. We are so blessed in this country. I declare it's time to maximize *every opportunity* to educate yourself on your craft or gifting.

On the other hand, some of us may not be as fortunate. For example, let's use the prophet Elisha here:

The prophet Elisha did not have all of these options. He didn't have the internet, social media, and other avenues that we often take for granted. From what we know, Elisha was a farmer. When Elijah found him after his encounter with God on Mount Horeb, the younger man *"was plowing with twelve yoke of oxen"* (**1 Kings 19:19 NIV**). There is no indication that Elisha had an extensive education or access to biblical scrolls or experience as a teacher or preacher. All Scripture tells us is that God charged Elijah, *"And Elisha the son of Shaphat from Abel of Meholah you shall anoint as prophet in your place"* (**1 Kings 19:16 NIV**).

What blesses me about this remarkable story is the fact that the prophet Elisha eliminated excuses. What are excuses, you ask? Excuses are, simply put, *"a crutch for those who are not really committed."* Unfortunately, we have a lot of people that want the gift or the office but are not willing to sacrifice for it. We need to see more examples of this in the Body of Christ, especially in the prophetic ministry.

Elisha was persistent and resilient. He didn't let people and things prevent him from his objective.

Most of us that operate in the prophetic are very familiar with this story. But I believe it should always be a source of reference, whether you are a prophet or not. At the end of the day, I don't care what your *mouth* says—what is it that your *actions* say? Your actions carry depth and volume which are much greater than what your mouth can ever express.

> *Remember, determination can accelerate your destiny…while a lack of determination can delay it.*

It's your call!

2 Kings 2:9-15 NIV

> *"When they had crossed, Elijah said to Elisha, 'Tell me, what can I do for you before I am taken from you?'*
>
> *'Let me inherit a double portion of your spirit,' Elisha replied.*
>
> *'You have asked a difficult thing,' Elijah said, 'yet if you see me when I am taken from you, it will be yours—otherwise, it will not.'*
>
> *As they were walking along and talking together, suddenly a chariot of fire and horses of fire appeared and separated the two of them, and Elijah went up to heaven in a whirlwind.*
>
> *Elisha saw this and cried out, 'My father! My father! The chariots and horsemen of Israel!' And Elisha saw him no more. Then he took hold of his garment and tore it in two.*
>
> *Elisha then picked up Elijah's cloak that had fallen from him and went back and stood on the bank of the Jordan.*
>
> *He took the cloak that had fallen from Elijah and struck the water with it. 'Where now is the Lord, the God of Elijah?' he asked. When he struck the water, it divided to the right and to the left, and he crossed over.*
>
> *The company of the prophets from Jericho, who were watching, said, 'The spirit of Elijah is resting on Elisha.' And they went to meet him and bowed to the ground before him."*

In my two decades or so of operating in the prophetic, I have come to the realization that a lot of people who propose to be "prophetic" are actually "dysfunctionally prophetic." This word *dysfunction* often occurs in one's life when one is distracted from the position and place of hearing God on behalf of the people as opposed to themselves. This person's gifts are often distorted because of their views, morals, and convictions. There is a certain degree or structure that they operate in.

People everywhere are being activated; however, this activation is just the beginning of their prophetic journey. We have become a prophetic society where the emphasis is on image and intelligence rather than on remaining grounded and stable. I really believe that with prophetic societies, we have to be cautious and remain vigilant, in order to not deviate from the principles of the prophetic. The prophet Balaam in **Numbers Chapter 22** and the prophet Gehazi in **2 Kings 5:21-27** were both guilty of this.

The spirit of error can be very misleading and deceptive if you don't have His Word deep in your heart. I have personally witnessed so many "prophetic social clubs" in the Body of Christ proclaim, "If you're not with us, you're against us!" That is absolutely absurd. There has to be a voice like John the Baptist's voice that is crying out in the wilderness of the prophetic madness and calling us back to order and balance.

We should be more concerned about building firm and strong prophetic voices and companies that are more interested in teaching and preparing each other to journey properly on our prophetic conquests. I sincerely believe one of the things on the heart of God in this season is for His prophets and prophetic ministry gifts to be more established, equipped, and exposed to His truths.

Proverbs 4:7 AMP

> *"The beginning of wisdom is: Get [skillful and godly] wisdom [it is preeminent]! And with all your acquiring, get understanding [actively seek spiritual discernment, mature comprehension, and logical interpretation]."*

Proverbs 11:1 AMP

"A false balance and dishonest business practices are extremely offensive to the Lord, but an accurate scale is His delight."

1 Corinthians 14:1-5 AMP

"Pursue [this] love [with eagerness, make it your goal], yet earnestly desire and cultivate the spiritual gifts [to be used by believers for the benefit of the Church], but especially that you may prophesy [to foretell the future, to speak a new message from God to the people]. For one who speaks in an unknown tongue does not speak to people but to God; for no one understands him or catches his meaning, but by the Spirit he speaks mysteries [secret truths, hidden things]. But [on the other hand] the one who prophesies speaks to people for edification [to promote their spiritual growth] and [speaks words of] encouragement [to uphold and advise them concerning the matters of God] and [speaks words of] consolation [to compassionately comfort them]. One who speaks in a tongue edifies himself; but one who prophesies edifies the Church [promotes growth in spiritual wisdom, devotion, holiness, and joy]. Now I wish that all of you spoke in unknown tongues, but even more [I wish] that you would prophesy. The one who prophesies is greater [and more useful] than the one who speaks in tongues, unless he translates or explains [what he says], so that the Church may be edified [instructed, improved, and strengthened]."

Ephesians 4:11-13 AMP

"And [His gifts to the Church were varied and] He Himself appointed some as apostles [special

messengers, representatives], some as prophets [who speak a new message from God to the people], some as evangelists [who spread the good news of salvation], and some as pastors and teachers [to shepherd, guide and instruct], [and He did this] to fully equip and perfect the saints (God's people) for works of service, to build up the Body of Christ [the church]; until we all reach oneness in the faith and in the knowledge of the Son of God, [growing spiritually] to become a mature believer, reaching to the measure of the fullness of Christ [manifesting His spiritual completeness and exercising our spiritual gifts in unity]."

Prophecy

I hear the Spirit of God saying, *"Your hibernating season is over! For My overlooked and disregarded prophets are coming out of the cave.*

For many of your gifts have been in hibernation, but I declare that God is activating and awakening the gift inside you.

For many of you have been under the radar; you've been out of sight. But did I not declare that the last shall be first?

For the light of My unprecedented favor is about to overshadow you.

For I will cause to rise in this hour, My Nathans.

For I will cause to rise in this hour, My Micaiahs.

For I will also cause to rise in this hour, My Shemaiahs.

For I will also cause to rise in this hour, My Huldahs…My Annas… yes even My Deborahs…and they shall come with great dimensions and demonstrations," says the Lord.

"For even those of you who have been under the attack of the enemy…

It's as if your gifts have been under attack, your calling has been under attack, your confidence has been under attack.

"Know this," says the Lord,

"It has been a spiritual conspiracy to destroy you, liken unto Haman.

For even as Haman built the gallows to destroy Mordecai, the very same gallows were used to take him out!

For that which was designed to destroy you, I will reverse it, and it shall explode on the enemy."

I declare that the Lord is taking out your Hamans.

I hear the Lord say, *"I'm breaking the hold of Haman over your assignment.*

For many of you have been in a place you cannot explain, a transition, for even the enemy would want to trap you in transition, but I have come that you might have life and have it more abundantly.

For many of you, the enemy has been running interference in your life because the influencer is rising on the inside of you, for the purpose of this interference was to intercept your assignment.

But behold, I give you the authority to excel and overthrow anything contrary to my will that stands in your way," says the Lord. *"Did I not say that greater is he that is within you?*

There is a level of greatness in you that's been trying to surface for some time now.

*Get ready, My sons and daughters, for the oil of overflow… overflow on your **gifts**…overflow on your **ministries**, overflow on your **finances**…for My glory shall fall and My anointing shall increase in you in this season.*

For even as we approach 2020, you will begin to move in and demonstrate optimum levels of the prophetic.

So, get ready, my influencers. Haman will not stop or block you this time!

Prophesy, prophesy, *and* **PROPHESY,** *I say!*

Stir up your gifts and allow My rivers to increase in you.

Build and don't look back, for there is much in store for you as you continue to trust me with your gifts," says the Lord.

Power Point 1

Prophetic Diversity

"Prophetic Diversity is developed through fellowship with the Holy Spirit, not through public personalities! You don't need to be a carbon copy of an original; be authentic and be the best you!"

Diversity denotes the state or fact of being diverse; difference; unlikeness; variety; multiformity.

When it comes down to flowing, functioning, and being free in your prophetic gift, you must understand that God deposited in all of us uniqueness. It is okay to be the one and only, but it's not okay to try to be someone else. The truth of the matter is, you may have experienced certain things to arrive at where you are currently.

> **Metron:** "staying in your lane," or "that which you are graced to function in."
>
> *"When you discover your Metron, you become a Magnet for Momentum, and with that Momentum comes the Money you need to advance the kingdom."*

At the end of the day, life is just so much better when you walk in your Metron!

The world is full of diversity. There are cultural differences, ethnic differences, economic differences, moral differences, value differences, and of course, religious differences. The point is, the world would be in a very unusual state if we were all the same. Diversity is what makes our nation such a great nation. We come together and unite if we are threatened by an adversary. We who are living in North America have so much to be thankful for.

I want to encourage you to lean in all the way and allow the Holy Spirit to lead and direct you. He will never steer you the wrong way. Diversity causes damage if it's misunderstood and wrongly applied. I declare that God is raising up prophetic warriors who will ignite and soar into what God has called them to be. Because at the end of the day, you can either be flourishing in your gift or just floating around with your gift and not landing in a safe place where you can be an original and not a copy. We have seen enough of the latent, "copy type" of people in the Church.

I challenge you to mount up, hit the runway, and get ready to be different in God. I promise you that He can handle it. People around you might not be able to, because you may disturb their insecurities. But God can handle it just fine!

Power Point 2

Beware of Deception in the Prophetic Ministry

"The prophetic without discernment is susceptible to deception and divination. Practice discernment and you'll develop longevity in the prophetic ministry."

The reality is that we should all want to be around doing what we love to do until it's our time to pass on the mantle. Associating with the right people can also help because you develop longevity in the prophetic ministry.

There are men and women of God who are generals and have been around for some time. They have developed a great degree of discernment on the subject of the prophetic. They have proven themselves and withstood the test of the times.

Deuteronomy 18:14-22 NIV

"The nations you will dispossess listen to those who practice sorcery or divination. But as for you, the Lord your God has not permitted you to do so. The Lord your God will raise up for you a prophet like me from among you, from your fellow Israelites. You must listen to him. For this is what you asked of the Lord your God at Horeb on the

day of the assembly when you said, 'Let us not hear the voice of the Lord our God nor see this great fire anymore, or we will die.'

The Lord said to me: 'What they say is good. I will raise up for them a prophet like you from among their fellow Israelites, and I will put my words in his mouth. He will tell them everything I command him. I myself will call to account anyone who does not listen to my words that the prophet speaks in my name. But a prophet who presumes to speak in my name anything I have not commanded, or a prophet who speaks in the name of other gods, is to be put to death.'

You may say to yourselves, 'How can we know when a message has not been spoken by the Lord?' If what a prophet proclaims in the name of the Lord does not take place or come true, that is a message the Lord has not spoken. That prophet has spoken presumptuously, so do not be alarmed."

Prophecy

"*I prophesy that the oil of heaven is about to saturate and soak the life and the heart of the prophet of God in this hour. I even hear that a greater depth of oil is about to be poured out, and the prophets on the rise in this hour will be distinguished from the profits. Get ready for portals of the prophetic to be unlocked and destinies released,*" says the Lord.

"*For I have longed to move in a providential way with my people and now the time is upon you, stir yourselves up and prophesy, for the fire that will emanate from you in this hour will be undeniable and unstoppable.*

Prophesy My word, prophesy in truth, and signs and miracles will manifest that destroy generational curses.

For My truth will carry you. My truth shall expose you to the gates of My glory. For My glory is where I reside, it's where increase resides and it's where favor resides. Tap in, tap in, and watch and see, for many rivers and streams will I open even unto thee.

My truth is stirring in my prophets.

My truth is stirring, so know indeed, for what I'm about to release on this movement will be unprecedented. This will even be one for the records.

A prophetic movement, a prophetic earthquake; so, get ready, the shaking has begun.

And there will even be several tremors on the east coast, west coast, and even north and south. A prophetic outbreak of clarity and truth shall be released in this hour," says the Lord.

> "One of the many reasons prophets get off track is because they are inconsistent with discernment. When you **discern** as a prophet, you **learn** as a prophet!"

Power Point 3

Three Major Essentials to the Prophetic Ministry

"Three major essentials to the prophetic ministry and the office of the Prophet: integrity, discernment, and love. Without these three, you are just really a person who profits."

Proverbs 10:9 NIV

*"Whoever walks in **integrity** walks securely, but whoever takes crooked paths will be found out."*

1 Kings 9:1-4 NIV

"When Solomon had finished building the temple of the Lord and the royal palace, and had achieved all he had desired to do, the Lord appeared to him a second time, as he had appeared to him at Gibeon. The Lord said to him:

'I have heard the prayer and plea you have made before me; I have consecrated this temple, which you have built, by putting My Name there forever. My eyes and my heart will always be there.

As for you, if you walk before me faithfully with integrity of heart and uprightness, as David your

> *father did, and do all I command and observe my decrees and laws, I will establish your royal throne over Israel forever, as I promised David your father when I said, "You shall never fail to have a successor on the throne of Israel."'*

We see here in this text how powerful integrity is. If we do our part, God will always make sure He does His part and honors His Word.

1 Corinthians 13:1-8 NIV

> *"If I speak in the tongues of men or of angels, but do not have love, I am only a resounding gong or a clanging cymbal. If I have the gift of prophecy and can fathom all mysteries and all knowledge, and if I have a faith that can move mountains, but do not have love, I am nothing. If I give all I possess to the poor and give over my body to hardship that I may boast, but do not have love, I gain nothing.*
>
> *Love is patient, love is kind. It does not envy, it does not boast, it is not proud. It does not dishonor others, it is not self-seeking, it is not easily angered, it keeps no record of wrongs. Love does not delight in evil but rejoices with the truth. It always protects, always trusts, always hopes, always perseveres.*
>
> *Love never fails. But where there are prophecies, they will cease; where there are tongues, they will be stilled; where there is knowledge, it will pass away."*

Love is what should really motivate every prophet and prophetic ministry gift. Love is the currency by which I believe the gift of prophecy is at its best. God Himself demonstrates this, Jesus the Son of God demonstrates this as well as many other biblical matriarchs and patriarchs.

1 Kings 3:11 NIV

> "So, God said to him, 'Since you have asked for this and not for long life or wealth for yourself, nor have asked for the death of your enemies but for **discernment** in administering justice.'"

2 Chronicles 2:12 NIV

> "And Hiram added: 'Praise be to the Lord, the God of Israel, who made heaven and earth! He has given King David a wise son, endowed with intelligence and **discernment**, who will build a temple for the Lord and a palace for himself.'"

Psalm 119:125 NIV

> "I am your servant; give me **discernment** that I may understand your statutes."

I want to highlight the word *discernment* because it is so essential for prophetic ministry development.

Discernment: the ability to judge well.

Synonyms: judgment, taste, discrimination, refinement, cultivation, sophistication, enlightenment, sensitivity, subtlety, insight, perception, perspicacity, perceptiveness, astuteness, acumen, shrewdness, ingeniousness, cleverness, intelligence, sharpness, wisdom, erudition, awareness, sagacity.

> "Discernment is not a matter of simply telling the difference between right and wrong; rather it is telling the difference between right and almost right."
>
> - Charles Spurgeon

Power Point 4

Prophets! You Must Know His Voice

"There are a lot of prophets that can quote a Scripture but quoting a Scripture doesn't verify that they can recognize His voice."
   "It is so very important to hear the right voice. Not everyone deserves your ear."

The Prophetic follows the acronym, **VOICE**. The prophetic tells us that:

- **V**ictory will be released in your life.
- **O**pportunities will arise in greater abundance in your life.
- **I**mposition: you will be called out of your comfort zone.
- **C**haracter: you will be strengthened to a higher level of character.
- **E**mbrace: you will conform to His will as you accept your assignment.

Wrong voices can **Derail** you, **Destroy** you, and **Distract** you while *right voices* can and will **Increase** you, **Impact** you, and **Inject** truth into your life.

You can *learn more* and *get more* out of life if you will invest more time in discovering the significance of having a *right voice* speak into your life…instead of just a *voice*. We see how Scriptures validate this statement. The children of Israel could not have been led by Aaron or Miriam, because God had chosen Moses. When it was time to cross over the Red Sea and escape from Pharaoh the oppressor, the people followed Moses' voice…because *he* followed the voice of the *Lord*.

The word *voice* carries much weight in the natural and spiritual realm. It releases volumes of directions and instructions for the people of God.

Isaiah 28:23 NIV

*"Listen and hear my **voice**; pay attention and hear what I say."*

Isaiah 30:21 NIV

*"Whether you turn to the right or to the left, your ears will hear a **voice** behind you, saying, 'This is the way; walk in it.'"*

John 10:27 NIV

*"My sheep listen to my **voice**; I know them, and they follow me."*

Power Point 5

Allow Him to Dress Your Prophetic Gift

"Become a mannequin for Him and allow Him to place on you His favor and might. Allow Him to dress you in His anointing so that authentic manifestations and miracles can occur."

John 2:27 NIV

> *"As for you, the **anointing** you received from him remains in you, and you do not need anyone to teach you. But as his **anointing** teaches you about all things and as that **anointing** is real, not counterfeit—just as it has taught you, remain in Him."*

Isaiah 10:27 AMP

> *"And it shall come to pass in that day, that his burden shall be taken away from off thy shoulder, and his yoke from off thy neck, and the yoke shall be destroyed because of the **anointing**."*

Luke 2:41-52 AMP

> *"Now His parents went to Jerusalem every year for the Passover Feast. And when He was twelve years old, they went up to Jerusalem, according to the custom of*

> the Feast; and as they were returning [to Nazareth], after spending the required number of days [at the Feast], the boy Jesus remained behind in Jerusalem. Now His parents did not know this, but supposed Him to be in the caravan, and traveled a day's journey; and [then] they began searching [anxiously] for Him among their relatives and acquaintances. When they did not find Him, they went back to Jerusalem looking for Him [everywhere]. Three days later they found Him in the [court of the] temple, sitting among the teachers, both listening to them and asking them questions. All who heard Him were amazed by His intelligence and His understanding and His answers. When they saw Him, they were overwhelmed; and His mother said to Him, 'Son, why have You treated us like this? Listen, your father and I have been [greatly distressed and] anxiously looking for You.' And He answered, 'Why did you have to look for Me? Did you not know that I had to be in My Father's house?' But they did not understand what He had said to them. He went down to Nazareth with them, and was continually submissive and obedient to them; and His mother treasured all these things in her heart.
>
> And Jesus kept increasing in wisdom and in stature, and in favor with God and men."

This story blesses me every time I read it. Jesus was willing to sacrifice and risk getting in trouble because inwardly, He knew that there was a great calling on His life. He knew that He must be about the Father's business even as a teenager. Of course, the end results were that He increased in favor with God and man.

Allow His anointing to rest on you. We actually sing songs like "Anointing Fall on Me." Well, I declare that we need to pull that song off the shelf, sing it, and mean it—wait until His anointing falls on you. This is how you can destroy yokes and make an impact in the kingdom.

Power Point 6

Prayer Ignites the Prophetic

"Prayer ignites the portal to the prophetic, reveals your passion for Him, pushes the button of purpose, and releases power to prosper in God's way."

One of the things that I have come to discover about the prophetic is that you can go so much further when you're equipped in prayer as opposed to just leaning on your gift.

I've personally been guilty of this, as I'm sure many others have. We can never allow prayer to be excluded from our prophetic lifestyle. The enemy would love to have prophets in the church without prayer. Prophets without consistent prayers become too open to hearing strange voices…voices other than the Lord's.

Prayer is that fire that lights the furnace of the prophetic.

Prayer is that vehicle that gets you to the appropriate destination.

Prayer is that wind that pushes things around in the Spirit and causes them to occur in the natural.

Prayer is that lifeline that keeps those of us in the prophetic ministry close to the heart of God.

Joel 1:13 AMP

> *"Clothe yourselves with sackcloth and lament (cry out in grief), O priests; Wail, O ministers of the altar! Come, spend the night in sackcloth [and **pray***

***without ceasing]**, O ministers of my God, For the grain offering and the drink offering are withheld from the house of your God."*

Colossians 4:2 AMP

*"Be persistent and devoted to **prayer**, being alert and focused in your **prayer** life with an attitude of thanksgiving."*

Jude 1:20 AMP

"But you, beloved, build yourselves up on [the foundation of] your most holy faith [continually progress, rise like an edifice higher and higher], pray in the Holy Spirit."

Power Point 7

The Elijah-Elisha Exchange

"Prophets, we must get a revelation of this principle called the Elijah-Elisha exchange. Without it, you can't expect to elevate if you don't eliminate pride. You can either settle in self, or soar into the double as God's Prophet."

Proverbs 11:2 AMP

> *"When **pride** comes [boiling up with an arrogant attitude of self-importance], then come dishonor and shame, but with the humble [the teachable who have been chiseled by trial and who have learned to walk humbly with God] there is wisdom and soundness of mind."*

Proverbs 16:18 AMP

> *"**Pride** goes before destruction, And a haughty spirit before a fall."*

As prophetic ministry gifts, we can learn a lot from the story of Elijah and Elisha. We see in this story how Elisha bows low to set himself up to be elevated high in God. Elisha knew that if he was going to grow in the prophetic, one of the first things he had to learn was to swallow his pride and submit to mentorship. This is a principle that must be applied; there are no discounts to promotion and elevation.

2 Kings 2:1–6 AMP

"When the Lord was about to take Elijah up to heaven by a whirlwind, Elijah and Elisha were traveling from Gilgal. And Elijah said to Elisha, 'Please stay here, for the Lord has sent me to Bethel.' But Elisha replied, 'As the Lord lives and as your soul lives, I will not leave you.' So, they went down to Bethel. Now the sons of the prophets who were at Bethel came out to Elisha and said to him, "Do you know that the Lord will take your master away from you today?' He said, 'Yes, I know it; be quiet [about it].'

Elijah said to him, 'Elisha, please stay here, for the Lord has sent me to Jericho.' But he said, 'As the Lord lives and as your soul lives, I will not leave you.' So they came to Jericho. The sons of the prophets who were at Jericho approached Elisha and said to him, 'Do you know that the Lord will take your master away from you today?' And he answered, 'Yes, I know it; be quiet [about it].' Elijah said to him, 'Please stay here, for the Lord has sent me to the Jordan.' But he said, 'As the Lord lives and as your soul lives, I will not leave you.' So the two of them went on."

Power Point 8

Serving a Prophetic Anointing Can Increase Yours

"Word of wisdom to the prophets and prophetic ministry gifts: You do not increase as you should in the anointing without serving someone else's anointing! There really is a biblical model and order to this."

One of my favorite examples is that of the story of Moses and Joshua. Moses had a past, he had a challenge in communication, and he had his own insecurities. However, through all of his hiccups and setbacks, Moses made up his mind that this was where he was supposed to be. People of God, you must know that you know who you are supposed to be connected to.

Where I sense that we often miss it is when we get caught up in a person's gift. What I love about this teaching moment is that not only was Joshua dedicated to the *person*, he was also dedicated to the *vision* of Moses. We don't see this too often in our churches, and when this occurs, people break off like a Paul-and-Barnabas situation—often because of something the two perhaps didn't see eye to eye on.

Churches would be so much more empowered in the prophetic anointing if we'd learn from others' mistakes in history and, simply put, don't repeat them.

Matthew 23:1-9 NIV

"Then Jesus said to the crowds and to his disciples: 'The teachers of the law and the Pharisees sit in Moses' seat. So you must be careful to do everything they tell you. But do not do what they do, for they do not practice what they preach. They tie up heavy, cumbersome loads and put them on other people's shoulders, but they themselves are not willing to lift a finger to move them.

Everything they do is done for people to see: They make their phylacteries wide and the tassels on their garments long; they love the place of honor at banquets and the most important seats in the synagogues; they love to be greeted with respect in the marketplaces and to be called "Rabbi" by others.

But you are not to be called "Rabbi," for you have one Teacher, and you are all brothers. And do not call anyone on earth "father," for you have one Father, and he is in heaven. Nor are you to be called instructors, for you have one Instructor, the Messiah. The greatest among you will be your servant. For those who exalt themselves will be humbled, and those who humble themselves will be exalted.'"

Too many people in this culture want the *position*, but not the *process*. Appreciation for an office or position can only be understood as we go through the process. The Church is full of believers who are half-and-half Christians. In other words, sometimes we serve God; then sometimes, when it's not convenient, we don't.

We see even in this text in **Matthew 23** that there were what the Bible describes as hypocrites. Anointings are not automatic! At some point, you will have to humble yourself and just submit to the process; because on the other side, there is promotion.

We are in a society where people want power and influence without sacrifice! That's a fool's perspective. For example, the supernatural doesn't occur without the right sacrifice. We need to build a culture of prophets and ministry gifts that are not caught up in a title or position. We need a culture where if we say we are prophets, let's be just that—prophets! Jesus himself dealt with this hypocritical spirit during His tenure. He understood firsthand how people's flesh can get in the way, and blind and block them from really maturing and flourishing in their gifts. This is what I want to call, "prophetic blind spots."

There are many people who are operating in distorted views as it relates to their prophetic gifts. What they often see has a lot to do with where they are currently positioned. This is why it is so important to stay in the right place—the place of humility and service. Humility will increase your gift, whereas pride or your unwillingness to comply will cause you to decrease in the grace and support of heaven.

These blind spots can occur when someone or something comes up on you and you don't see it perhaps until it's too late. Blind spots often occur when you're in motion in your car. If you're not cautious, sometimes, it can destroy or damage you at the blink of an eye. This is why driving instructions emphasize that you should always make sure your mirrors are set! To get to where God has asked you to go will require you to make sure your mirrors are set right. So, the next time you look in the mirror, my prayer is that you see Christ. It is truly a blessing in serving others. Never allow the enemy to take that passion and posture from you.

Power Point 9

Don't Disconnect from Divine Appointments

"The deception of the enemy is always to cause you to naturally disconnect from a divine prophetic appointment and mentorship moment to abort your spiritual assignment."

Mentorship: *"Allowing someone the consent to journey through life with you until you reach your prophetic destiny."*

The world is full of tactics and schemes to attempt to pull you away from whom you're supposed to be connected to. Social media, television, friends and family, jobs, and careers can be devices the enemy will use to disconnect you from your Moses moment.

There are several classifications of individuals I want to address here:

There's the **partially connected** person.

This person is sometimes "feeling it" and sometimes "not feeling it." One day, he is a prophet; and then the next day, he isn't, for whatever reason. He also struggles with the will of his flesh and his identity. He might be doing perhaps just enough to appease people. His prophetic gift is often subject to personal whims: *"If this is convenient for me, I'll do it,"* or *"If there's nothing in it for me, then why should I even consider doing this?"* Just wanting overall to do it his way and not consider or regard the consequences or the damage it could do to others.

There's the **phony-connected** individual.

This individual is just like the Scripture says, having the presentation of, but not really engrafted in the Word, the prophetic anointing, and his assignment.

2 Timothy 3:5 AMP

> "...holding to a form of [outward] godliness (religion), although they have denied its power [for their conduct nullifies their claim of faith]. Avoid such people and keep far away from them."

There's the **popularity-connected** individual.

This person thrives off of the excitement of the crowd. He often connects for the sake of fame and notoriety. Most of the time, it only matters really what's in it for him. He often attempts to connect with big-name individuals to help him feel and look like he has arrived. Often, just like in the TV series "Cheers," sometimes, you want to go where everybody knows your name. Ironically, the Church is full of superficial and artificial Christians. Prophetic gifts who live for the attention and the limelight—having their name on the flyers and being the special guest at some conference—there is a lot of immaturity that is present in this particular person.

There's the **privately connected** person.

This person associates with specific people when others perhaps may not be around. He doesn't often like to be identified as one who is connected with a certain individual. So, he tries to keep it secret. Perhaps he's unsure of his assignment or he simply doesn't want everyone to know that he is connected to a certain person.

There's the **purpose-connected** individual.

This individual accepts the call and is willing to endure whatever comes along in the process. He understands that this is destiny that has brought us together. He is willing to stay connected because everything he has gone through has equipped him for this season of preparation. Perhaps there's a lesson here in the story of Ruth and Naomi, in **Ruth Chapter 1**.

Ruth 1:14-18 AMP

> *"Then they wept aloud again; and Orpah kissed her mother-in-law [goodbye], but Ruth clung to her.*
>
> *Then Naomi said, 'Look, your sister-in-law has gone back to her people and to her gods; turn back and follow your sister-in-law.' But Ruth said, 'Do not urge me to leave you or to turn back from following you; for where you go, I will go, and where you lodge, I will lodge. Your people will be my people, and your God, my God. Where you die, I will die, and there I will be buried. May the Lord do the same to me [as He has done to you], and more also, if anything but death separates me from you.' When Naomi saw that Ruth was determined to go with her, she said nothing more."*

This is an amazing example of someone willing to let go of their past and present to believe that "if I leave with you, I'll have a better future." Ruth makes a strong confession or statement, and as a result of being purposely connected, she met her Boaz.

Now let's focus on another aspect of connection in conjunction to community. We see the significance of this in Scripture, from Moses and the children of Israel, to Samuel and his school of prophets, and the Apostle Paul and those with whom he mentored and had community with. The results are so much more beneficial as opposed to just being part-time relational.

This is why it's so important to establish a prophetic community. No one really likes feeling like an outsider, but the fact of the matter is that people do feel that way often! Community is what helps build people, affirms people, encourages people, and increases the value of the people. Unfortunately, we don't have enough of this in the Church today, because everyone's concerned about growing their ministries.

If you notice the root word in *community* is *commune*, which is defined as: *to converse or talk together, usually with profound intensity, intimacy, etc.; interchange thoughts or feelings.*

There will always be something or someone speaking in your ear to go here: *"Don't stay there; Come be with us;"* and *"I sense the Lord wants you to connect with us."* We see this displayed with Eve in the Garden of Eden.

Now I believe that when it comes to this, it should be confirmed by both parties. Both should have a definitive witness. Because people will do their best to increase themselves at your expense!

People all over the Body of Christ are now starting what we call "prophetic hubs." My question is this: *What provoked or led you to establish a tribe?* Saints, let's be real here—every prophetic tribe is not being led by the Spirit of God! The soul in some instances takes the steering wheel and determines that if you don't have money, the looks, the swag, and the social media presence, then we'll go with someone else. A lot of so-called "decisions" are made by flesh and not by the faith we should have in God's Word!

Prophetic communities are so needed in our culture. People want more than a one-sided relationship. Let me just define this word, *community.*

Community: *a feeling of fellowship with others, as a result of sharing common attitudes, interests, and goals.*

a unified body of individuals

a group of people with a common characteristic or interest living together within a larger society.

Synonyms for community *would be population, brotherhood, association, colony, company, group, body, sect, or band.*

I believe that if we can build stronger prophetic communities, we'll see less people being enticed, tricked, and deceived to disconnect prematurely. Not all departing is bad, some hubs you just need to run from, as Joseph ran from Potiphar's wife. But if we are going to develop stronger, more stable and sound prophets and prophetic ministry gifts, we must learn once again from the model of Jesus.

As long as I can remember, there has always been something that is assigned to assassinate your assignment. Understand this, that whenever you begin to evolve into what God has called you to be, you will always deal with an adversary. There will always be what I call, "Traps in Transition." The enemy would love to confuse many of us who are in transition. Transition here implies that you are coming into your gifting, your appetite is increasing, and your passion is undeniable. This is when the enemy would love to trick you with things such as frustration: they don't understand I'm called to, they are too controlling, and they don't honor or regard me and care if I even exist. All of these are signs that can cause catastrophe if they remain misguided and unchecked.

I want to highlight here a particular story with the Apostle Paul and Barnabas that I believe we can all learn from. They were two men of God who had a mandate to preach the gospel. They were distinct, different, and determined. Barnabas was more so the senior or elder one, and Paul was the younger of the two.

Sometime later, Paul said to Barnabas, *"Let us go back and visit the believers in all the towns where we preached the Word of the Lord and see how they are doing."* Barnabas wanted to take John (also called Mark) with them, but Paul did not think it was wise to take him, because he had deserted them in Pamphylia and had not continued with them in the work. They had such a sharp disagreement that they parted company. Barnabas took Mark and sailed for Cyprus, but Paul chose Silas and left, commended by the believers to the grace of the Lord. He went through Syria and Cilicia, strengthening the churches.

Now there is no definitive as to exactly what may have really transpired. All we read here is that Paul chose Silas, and it was implied rather abruptly here. However, it is assumed it wasn't so much as a doctrine belief as of why they parted ways, but more so some personal thing or a sort of disagreement. Of course, for those of us familiar, we know that there was another individual involved here by the name of John Mark. Barnabas wanted to have John Mark travel with them, I believe just right before Paul's second missionary journey, but Paul thought otherwise. Now what's amazing about this story is that they were both spiritual men, on fire for God. They knew their identities, but that doesn't mean they were exempt from having a spirit intruding and running interference in their relationship. It is so important in our relationships that we do our best to guard them. Somewhere along the way, one of the two or both of them opened the door to disconnection.

Paul had three missionary trips; during which he wrote sixty to seventy-five percent of the New Testament. The Bible continues to talk about his challenges as well as his victories; but Barnabas, you really never heard of him again after they disconnected. I believe that in the words *connect* and *disconnect*, they both involve the word *timing*! This is so vital in ministry, in whatever aspect you're involved in.

For example, when you're landing a plane, it requires the timing to be right; and when you're preparing to take off, it requires the component of timing as well to be right. There is no way around the timing of the Lord. However, people find an illegitimate way all the time. They move or step out and start a ministry without the consultation and confirmation of the Lord. I don't have all the answers as of why their relationship dissolved, but this thing is so prevalent in our churches—from people that leave too soon, to those who stayed and sowed discord. Here again, we can learn from Jesus as the prime example of the One who dealt respectively with transitions. Jesus touched every facet of the five-fold ministry. He even laid it out for us and taught the disciples three things to maintain balance in your life: *fasting*, *praying*, and *giving*. These three things Jesus emphasized to his followers, and here again, it helped build community.

I have to keep referring to Jesus prior to His Resurrection—Mary Magdalene visited his tomb only to discover he was gone. The powerful thing about this illustration is that every ministerial gift, congregant, or member of a church can learn from this. Jesus actually took the time and folded his linen as if to say, *"Make sure you leave a place in proper order or the right way!"* We have to get back to this place in the Church.

Proverbs 6:16–19 KJV

> *"These six things doth the Lord hate: yea, seven are an abomination unto him:*

> *A proud look, a lying tongue, and hands that shed innocent blood,*
>
> *An heart that deviseth wicked imaginations, feet that be swift in running to mischief,*
>
> *A false witness that speaketh lies, and he that soweth discord among brethren."*

"There are three major reasons why people often disconnect or separate: doctrine, sin, or discord."
 ~Apostle Johnathan Stidham

As pastors and leaders, most of us have encountered this to some extent. But believe me, God *is* and *will always be* a God of order. It's always to your advantage to be in His timing. Understand that at the end of the day, God may have scheduled you for a test, but the enemy has also planned traps for you!

Ecclesiastes 3:1-9, 11 KJV

> *"To everything there is a season, and a time to every purpose under the heaven:*
>
> *A time to be born, and a time to die; a time to plant, and a time to pluck up that which is planted;*
>
> *A time to kill, and a time to heal; a time to break down, and a time to build up;*
>
> *A time to weep, and a time to laugh; a time to mourn, and a time to dance;*
>
> *A time to cast away stones, and a time to gather stones together; a time to embrace, and a time to refrain from embracing;*
>
> *A time to get, and a time to lose; a time to keep, and a time to cast away;*

A time to rend, and a time to sew; a time to keep silence, and a time to speak;

A time to love, and a time to hate; a time of war, and a time of peace."

He hath made everything beautiful in His time; also, He hath set the world in their heart, so that no man can find out the work that God maketh from the beginning to the end.

I believe with all my heart that whomever God has called you to connect to will happen. You don't have to force it or "help expedite it." Don't be one of those Christians that puts the carriage before the horse, when in reality, it was designed to go the other way around. Whereas the horses go out front before the carriage, the carriage would be very difficult to move when it's out of order. So is your prophetic gift when you don't allow it to mature the correct way.

Now if you're reading this and you are thinking that you may have disconnected from your God-set place, know that you are not beyond restoration. We have had people leave our ministry, but later realized that their set place was with us.

Let me just take another moment to build your faith and encourage you here. You don't have to spend your life in guilt, condemnation, or regret. If you left a certain place, own up to it—repent, shake it off, and go back home.

There are four things we should gather from a scenario such as this:

1. The decisions of our past don't have to determine our future.
2. If you fall short in any area relative to your assignment, never feel that God cannot still use you.
3. It's never too late to reconnect after you've prematurely disconnected.
4. As long as there is breath in your body, you still have time to forgive.

Power Point 10

The Prophetic Is Not an Excuse to Be in Error

"The prophetic is not an excuse to be off and in error. The prophetic stays always on track with truth. Order is always part of the assignment of the prophetic. Practice it and you'll see."

We have learned and been taught time and time again that an excuse is really at some point a crutch for the uncommitted.

Proverbs 9:8 AMP

> *"Do not correct a scoffer [who foolishly ridicules and takes no responsibility for his **error**] or he will hate you; Correct a wise man [who learns from his **error**], and he will love you."*

Isaiah 32:6 AMP

> *"For the fool speaks nonsense, and his heart (mind) plans wickedness: To practice ungodliness and to speak **error** concerning the Lord, To keep the craving of the hungry unsatisfied And to deprive the thirsty of drink."*

Matthew 24:4 AMP

*"Jesus answered, 'Be careful that no one misleads you [deceiving you and leading you into **error**].'"*

2 Timothy 3:16 AMP

*"All Scripture is God-breathed [given by divine inspiration] and is profitable for instruction, for conviction [of sin], for correction [of **error** and restoration to obedience], for training in righteousness [learning to live in conformity to God's will, both publicly and privately—behaving honorably with personal integrity and moral courage]..."*

Titus 1:9 AMP

*"He must hold firmly to the trustworthy word [of God] as it was taught to him, so that he will be able both to give accurate instruction in sound [reliable, **error**-free] doctrine and to refute those who contradict [it by explaining their **error**]."*

2 Peter 3:16 AMP

*"...speaking about these things as he does in all of his letters. In which there are some things that are difficult to understand, which the untaught and unstable [who have fallen into **error**] twist and misinterpret, just as they do the rest of the Scriptures, to their own destruction."*

1 John 4:6 AMP

"We [who teach God's word] are from God [energized by the Holy Spirit], and whoever knows God [through personal experience] listens to us [and has a deeper understanding of Him]. Whoever is

> *not of God does not listen to us. By this we know [without any doubt] the spirit of truth [motivated by God] and the spirit of **error** [motivated by Satan]."*

I put several Scriptures here on error because it has become a major epidemic in the Church. There's often a lot of prophecy that can't be backed up biblically. As prophetic gifts, we must keep in mind that once you open the door of error, you are right down the hallway to divination.

I see this so often in the prophetic ministry—no one wants their words judged or even screened by their peers. This becomes what I call, "the breeding ground for Endor." The Bible talks of a place called Endor where all the mediums, witches, warlocks, and physicians went during the reign of Israel's first king, Saul, in **1 Samuel Chapter 28**.

Power Point 11

Prophecy Is Not Based on a Hunch

"Prophecy is not based on a feeling, a supposition, an inference, a calculated guess, or even sanctified wisdom. Prophecy is the human report of a divine revelation or inspiration, the forth-telling or the foretelling of a matter. This is what distinguishes and separates prophecy from teaching. Teaching is always grounded in an inspired text of Scripture. Prophecy, on the other hand, is always based on a spontaneous revelation, distributed as the Spirit of God wills or what we often refer to as a Rhema or right now word."

Prophecy in its simplistic form is just the currency of the prophetic that is led and inspired by the Spirit of God. Prophecy is not just something that is—it connects the dots from the past to the present and to the future.

2 Peter 1:21 AMP

> *"...or no **prophecy** was ever made by an act **of** human will, but men moved by the Holy **Spirit** spoke from God."*

Revelation 19:10 AMP

*"Then I fell down at his feet to worship him, but he [stopped me and] said to me, 'You must not do that; I am a fellow servant with you and your brothers and sisters who have and hold the testimony **of** Jesus. Worship God [alone]. For the testimony **of** Jesus is the **spirit of prophecy** [His life and teaching are the heart **of prophecy**].'"*

Power Point 12

A Prophet's Journey in the Word

"Prophets need to constantly take more of a journey in the Word and less in the world."

I have learned from experience to make sure that as a prophetic ministry gift, you become more familiar with the Word than you do your gift. Your gift only goes so far; but with the Word infused and engrafted in your heart, you'll reach optimum levels in the prophetic.

Psalm 119:105 AMP

> *"Your **word** is a lamp to my feet and a light to my path."*

Psalm 119:30 KJV

> *"The entrance of thy **words** giveth light; it giveth understanding unto the simple."*

John 1:1 AMP

> *"In the beginning [before all-time] was the **Word** (Christ), and the **Word** was with God, and the **Word** was God Himself."*

As prophets, you cannot effectively judge a prophetic release, a prophetic word, or prophecy if your word content is deficient.

For example, if your body doesn't have the appropriate nutrients it needs, then it will not produce at its maximum capacity. The gift of prophecy should be demonstrated at its best, to bless the life of the people of God on a regular basis. Unfortunately, we see many people that are functioning in the office or title of a prophet, but who are dysfunctional, deficient, dislocated, and disconnected from the revelation of the Word of God. Notice how the prophets in the Old Testament were based and balanced to a degree in the Word that kept them constantly increasing in their respective gifts.

The culture of the modern Church has so much that we've often strayed away from as it relates to our gifts. We are in such a society that's commercially driven and not consciously driven. It tends to be more about comparison and competition, and not about character as it relates to ministry.

Proverbs 22:28 KJV

"Remove not the ancient landmark, which thy fathers have set."

Solomon gives us great advice and wisdom here as it relates to that which has already been established. For us as prophetic ministry gifts, there is order that's required which keeps us in check and balanced.

The Word should become automatic for us as prophets as we spend time with the Father. You shouldn't have to force yourself into it—your love for the Word should be natural. You know when something is off in your life when it becomes difficult to get in the Word of God. Of course, the devil would love this so that perversion and other displays of error can manifest in your life. But I want to implore and encourage you, find some time for the Word and less for the world, and God will give you the world—in that order.

Power Point 13

Prophets Develop Their Gift in the Dark Room

"Prophets must develop in the dark room where people can't see them, not always in public. The real you will eventually surface, depending on which one you desire to grow in, the public eye or the private, in God's eyes."

1 Timothy 4:16 AMP

*"Pay close attention to yourself [concentrate on your personal **development**] and to your teaching; persevere in these things [hold to them], for as you do this you will ensure salvation both for yourself and for those who hear you."*

James 1:4 AMP

*"And let endurance have its perfect result and do a thorough work, so that you may be perfect and completely **developed** [in your faith], lacking in nothing."*

Matthew 6:6 AMP

> *"But when you pray, go into your most private room, close the door and pray to your Father who is **in secret**, and your Father who sees [what is done] **in secret** will reward you."*

It is so important that as prophetic gifts, we allow the appropriate channels and outlets for God to prep us, train us, and position us. The fact of the matter is, everything that glitters in the public eye is not gold. There are a lot of gold-plated prophets—they look the part, act the part, and even dress the part.

One of the tests of a true prophet is that you learn how to go low and sit before you can stand up. In other words, having the mic first without being developed can be dangerous. But unfortunately, we see a lot of this in the Church—people being handed the title or the office of a prophet with no time invested in the trenches. Please be careful who you deem a prophet—they just might not be mentally, emotionally, physically, and spiritually ready.

As prophets, we develop more so that we spend more time in His face than in the face of man. I believe there's always a lesson to learn—whether by your vocation, career, job, or the church you attend—there are always reasons for learning and listening. When you do this, you develop into one who is leveled and who will have longevity in the prophetic ministry.

Power Point 14

Requirements for the Prophetic

"Prophetic requirements for prophetic gifts:"

Have an undeniable *Passion* for the prophetic
Understanding its *Purpose*
Their lifeline is *Prayer* and the Word
Processes through Discernment
Pursuit of His *presence* and Word
Understanding the *Prophetic Code of Ethics*
Mentorship by *Proven* Gifts
Being *Planted* in a stable house or church
Having no room for *Pride*

Things that I need to prophesy:

1. Understand what prophecy is and what it's not
2. I must have faith
3. I must be a student of the Word
4. Have an ear to hear
5. A strong desire to prophesy
6. A mentor
7. A covering
8. Humility

Power Point 15

Don't Dilute the Truth of the Prophetic

"False prophets are artificial. They dilute the truth and deceive, while true prophets are authentic. They always give birth to truth."

Exodus 18:21 AMP

> *"Furthermore, you shall select from all the people competent men who [reverently] fear God, men of **truth**, those who hate dishonest gain; you shall place these over the people as leaders of thousands, of hundreds, of fifties and of tens."*

Job 17:12 AMP

> *"These [thoughts try to] make the night into the day; 'The light is near,' they say in the presence of darkness [but they pervert the **truth**].*
>
> *As long as there is the gift of prophecy or present **truth** in the church, the enemy will always try to pervert or twist it. This is one main reason why we need established prophets that will train and teach."*

John 8:32 AMP

> "And you will know the truth [regarding salvation], and the truth will set you free [from the penalty of sin]."

John 16:13 AMP

> "But when He, the **Spirit of Truth**, comes, He will guide you into all the truth [full and complete **truth**]. For He will not speak on His own initiative, but He will speak whatever He hears [from the Father—the message regarding the Son], and He will disclose to you what is to come [in the future]."

A great example of a prophet that errored intentionally would be that of the prophet Hananiah in the Book of Jeremiah.

> "But shortly after the prophet Hananiah had broken the yoke off the prophet Jeremiah's neck, the Lord spoke to Jeremiah. 'Go and tell Hananiah that the Lord says, "You have indeed broken the wooden yoke. But you have only succeeded in replacing it with an iron one! For the Lord God of Israel who rules overall says, 'I have put an irresistible yoke of servitude on all these nations so they will serve King Nebuchadnezzar of Babylon. And they will indeed serve him. I have even given him control over the wild animals.' Then the prophet Jeremiah told the prophet Hananiah, 'Listen, Hananiah! The Lord did not send you! You are making these people trust in a lie! So, the Lord says, 'I will most assuredly remove you from the face of the earth. You will die this very year because you have counseled rebellion against the Lord.' In the seventh month of that very same year the prophet Hananiah died." (**Jeremiah 28:12-17**)

God charges Hananiah with causing the people to trust in a lie, as well as inciting rebellion against Him. His transgressions were so grievous that God killed Hananiah two months later—a month for each year in his false vision.

Hananiah's prophecy urged rebellion against God in a couple of ways. First, Scripture is clear that God had installed Nebuchadnezzar in a position of power over the known world. Though not a godly man, he filled a position that God had given him, thus, to resist his rule was to rebel against the God-ordained order. When Hananiah predicted deliverance in just two years, it encouraged Judeans to think that they did not have to submit to this foreign king. In this way, he encouraged them to disregard God-instituted authority.

Second, Hananiah's lie subtly altered the reason for their crisis. He redefined the foreign domination from something that God deliberately caused (as told by the prophets) into something that He merely allowed and would soon remedy. The false prophet shifted the explanation of their pitiful circumstances from something that God had orchestrated due to the sins of His people into a time-and-chance problem that He would reverse.

This removed any need for self-examination. It exonerated the nation and its leaders, removing any thought that the people had misbehaved themselves into this crisis by rejecting God. By eliminating any thought of cause-and-effect regarding sin, Hananiah was in fact encouraging them to continue in their disobedience. Without any apparent consequences for sin, the mind begins to reason that sin is not the problem. Hananiah told them everything would be fine, but God saw it as teaching His people to rebel.

This is something that we see in other instances as well, such as Gehazi and Balaam, even with our modern-day millennial prophets and prophetic gifts. The line of deception can appear very thin; but once you open the door, you may never know the extent of what spirits you invite in. The Bible states that it's the small fox that destroys the vine.

Song of Solomon 2:15 NIV

"Catch for us the foxes, the little foxes that ruin the vineyards, our vineyards that are in bloom."

Hananiah the prophet found out firsthand that you cannot intentionally get away with deceiving the people of God.

Proverbs 16:25 NIV

"There is a way that appears to be right, but in the end it leads to death."

Twelve Examples of False Prophets:

Ahab in **Jeremiah 29:21**
Anti-Christ in **1 John 2:18-19**
Azur in **Jeremiah 28:1**
Balaam in **Numbers Chapters 22-25**
Elymas, better known as Bar-Jesus, in **Acts 13:6-12**
Hananiah in **Jeremiah 28:5**
Jezebel in **Revelation 2:20** (not to be confused with the Jezebel in the Old Testament)
A false prophet in **Revelation 16:13, 19:20, 20:10**
The false prophets of Baal in **1 Kings 18:13-40**
Noadiah in **Nehemiah 6:14**
Simon Magus in **Acts 8:9-24**
Zedekiah in **Jeremiah 29:21** and **1 Kings 22:24**

Power Point 16

Plant Your Gift so Your Roots Can Grow

"When it comes to the prophetic, there is no tree that's willing to stand alone except when it has roots. Allow your gift to get planted and grow some before you call yourself a prophet."

This particular point is so important to those of us in the prophetic ministry. We are in a time right now where there is a "Nomad Spirit" on the prophetic gifts. A *nomad* is defined as *a drifter, one who doesn't set up camp for long, but eventually wanders or drifts off to the next place.*

I believe that if we're going to be prophetic gifts, let's be just that! Get planted and grow some roots so you can have greater credibility than just your word. Think about in the secular setting they have that is called the workplace. Well, the workplace that you may try to get employed at will require some type of references and previous job history. Here's one aspect that I believe the Church really needs to glean from. We have learned from experience that you inspect what you expect!

I have had to counsel individuals who have invited prophets and so-called apostles into their churches and then they were destroyed with division and discord. Just because a person says he or she is an apostle or prophet doesn't mean you just have to accept it. I know this may be a little strong for some people, but facts are facts! You have every God-given right to research, inspect, check their social media accounts— hey, whatever it takes.

Here's one Scripture that I know some prophets and prophetic gifts struggle with. I get very concerned when prophets particularly don't feel as though they need to be planted in someone's church. I believe there's a blessing of favor and increase that you will become exposed to when you are submitted, covered, and planted. A tree can never really serve its purpose and last except when it is planted and has allowed its roots to run deep.

Psalm 1:3 AMP

> *"And he will be like a tree firmly **planted** [and fed] by streams of water, which yields its fruit in its season; Its leaf does not wither; And in whatever he does, he prospers [and comes to maturity]."*

Psalm 92:12-15 KJV

> *"The righteous shall flourish like the palm tree: he shall grow like a cedar in Lebanon.*
>
> *Those that be planted in the house of the Lord shall flourish in the courts of our God.*
>
> *They shall still bring forth fruit in old age; they shall be fat and flourishing;*
>
> *To shew that the Lord is upright: he is my rock, and there is no unrighteousness in him."*

1 John 3:24 AMP

> *"The one who habitually keeps His commandments [obeying His word and following His precepts, **abides** and] remains **in Him**, and He **in him**. By this we know and have the proof that He [really] **abides in** us, by the Spirit whom He has given us [as a gift]."*

Power Point 17

Prophetic Objectives

"When it often comes to the prophetic, some prophets miss out on the objective and the assignment. The office of the prophet is a lifetime calling to build up the Body, not for just when you want an offering."

Proverbs 4:7 AMP

> *"The beginning of wisdom is: Get [skillful and godly] wisdom [it is preeminent]! And with all your acquiring, get understanding [actively seek spiritual discernment, mature comprehension, and logical interpretation]. When one accepts the call to walk in the office of the prophet or either the prophetic ministry, there must always be clarifications of the assignment. If one doesn't have the understanding, you will be headed right towards devastation."*

Paul instructs the Corinthian Church on the matter rather extensively. I believe that after his God encounter, he became very driven for the things of God with a relentless passion.

1 Corinthians 14:1-5 AMP

> *"Pursue [this] love [with eagerness, make it your goal], yet earnestly desire and cultivate the*

spiritual gifts [to be used by believers for the benefit of the Church], but especially that you may prophesy [to foretell the future, to speak a new message from God to the people]. For one who speaks in an unknown tongue does not speak to people but to God; for no one understands him or catches his meaning, but by the Spirit he speaks mysteries [secret truths, hidden things]. But [on the other hand] the one who prophesies speaks to people for edification [to promote their spiritual growth] and [speaks words of] encouragement [to uphold and advise them concerning the matters of God] and [speaks words of] consolation [to compassionately comfort them]. One who speaks in a tongue edifies himself; but one who prophesies edifies the Church [promotes growth in spiritual wisdom, devotion, holiness, and joy]. Now I wish that all of you spoke in unknown tongues, but even more [I wish] that you would prophesy. The one who prophesies is greater [and more useful] than the one who speaks in tongues, unless he translates or explains [what he says], so that the Church may be edified [instructed, improved, strengthened]."

The prophetic ministry has an objective to assist in building up and assisting in one's constructional process relative to their destiny, to draw them near to their calling and provoke them to their purpose, and lastly, to release a degree of clarity and eliminate all of the confusion and second guessing of one's purpose.

The gift of prophecy really has to be instructed more in our churches and not just demonstrated. There is a need to establish teams in the Church and inform believers that they too can prophesy the Word of the Lord.

Somewhere along the way, when there's not a revelation on the prophetic gift, people will often abuse and mishandle it.

Now, when it comes to the assignment component, I believe God set this gift in the Church to help decode and unlock to sentiments of our hearts, help us in connecting the dots, and making sense out of things. The assignment of the prophetic is so vital and key to the Church's increasing and enlarging.

Power Point 18

Listening and Learning Lead to Longevity

"In the prophetic, listening and learning lead to longevity and as you trust Him, He will keep you away from lies."

I have learned over the years that as a prophet, you have to learn how to listen much more than you speak. Real prophets know prophesying doesn't always define you as a prophet. Think about this—God gave us all two ears and one mouth. Now you figure that one out!

Solomon, one of the wisest men that there was, asked for wisdom above all else.

1 Kings 3:4-15 NIV

> *"The king went to Gibeon to offer sacrifices, for that was the most important high place, and Solomon offered a thousand burnt offerings on that altar. At Gibeon the Lord appeared to Solomon during the night in a dream, and God said, 'Ask for whatever you want me to give you.' Solomon answered, 'You have shown great kindness to your servant, my father David, because he was faithful to you and righteous and upright in heart. You have continued this great*

kindness to him and have given him a son to sit on his throne this very day.

Now, Lord my God, you have made your servant king in place of my father David. But I am only a little child and do not know how to carry out my duties. Your servant is here among the people you have chosen, a great people, too numerous to count or number. So, give your servant a discerning heart to govern your people and to distinguish between right and wrong. For who is able to govern this great people of yours?'

The Lord was pleased that Solomon had asked for this. So God said to him, 'Since you have asked for this and not for long life or wealth for yourself, nor have asked for the death of your enemies but for discernment in administering justice, I will do what you have asked. I will give you a wise and discerning heart, so that there will never have been anyone like you, nor will there ever be. Moreover, I will give you what you have not asked for—both wealth and honor—so that in your lifetime you will have no equal among kings. And if you walk in obedience to me and keep my decrees and commands as David your father did, I will give you a long life.' Then Solomon awoke—and he realized it had been a dream.

He returned to Jerusalem, stood before the ark of the Lord's covenant and sacrificed burnt offerings and fellowship offerings. Then he gave a feast for all his court."

Proverbs 3:1-6 AMP

"My son, do not forget my teaching, But let your heart keep my commandments; For length of days and years of life [worth living] And tranquility and

prosperity [the wholeness of life's blessings] they will add to you. Do not let mercy and kindness and truth leave you [instead let these qualities define you]; Bind them [securely] around your neck, Write them on the tablet of your heart. So, find favor and high esteem in the sight of God and man. Trust in and rely confidently on the Lord with all your heart and do not rely on your own insight or understanding.

In all your ways know and acknowledge and recognize Him, And He will make your paths straight and smooth [removing obstacles that block your way]."

Power Point 19

Strange Fire

"Not all prophetic fire is from God. The supernatural is not always a sign of God. It could be a work of man disguised as spiritual. Beware of strange fire."

Leviticus 10:1 AMP

> *"[The Sin of Nadab and Abihu] Now Nadab and Abihu, the sons of Aaron, took their respective [ceremonial] censers, put **fire** in them, placed incense on it and offered **strange** (unauthorized, unacceptable) **fire** before the Lord, [an act] which He had not commanded them to do. As prophetic ministry gifts, we must understand that just because it sounds like a prophet doesn't necessarily mean that it is. I tell people all the time, everything that may be prophetic may not be relative or prevalent for you. You have to be able to accept this and be okay with it."*

The Church is full of all kinds of strange fire. It's going to take prophets that have the heart of God and who are able to see in the Spirit to expose strange fire for what it is—strange fire. There are all kinds of stirrings in the Body of Christ. Just as there is a doctrine of truth, there is also a doctrine of error. I have encountered some very interesting situations to say the least in the church world.

There's a fire of the flesh. This is when flesh goes on a parade to divert attention away from God. For example, the presence of the Lord can be present and moving; and then all of a sudden, a person gets loud, unruly, and inconsiderate. They may jump up and shout or run, or even cause a dramatic scene, and believe me, I've seen a lot of this in church. A lot of times, people get caught up in the emotions or hype of church. Strange fire is when the passion tends to be misguided or misinterpreted. Another example would be when the pastor is up preaching and someone jumps up; and because of this fire, which they say is burning on the inside, they feel as though they must share what they think is the Word of Lord. Now I'm not saying this is always the case, but there always has to be order in the house!

Power Point 20

The Prophetic Connects Your Heart and Mind to Purpose

"The prophetic has the anointing and the ability to connect your mouth, mind, and purpose with the mind and heart of God."

As believers, we can benefit tremendously from the prophetic gift.

1 Corinthian 12:7 KJV

> *"But the manifestation of the Spirit is given to every man to profit withal."*

Let's look at the story of David prior to becoming king. The prophet Samuel gets the Word of the Lord to go and anoint the next king of Israel. David is somewhere, tending to the sheep in the field. And one thing we all can learn from David was that he was a man after the heart of God. He receives the prophetic word and the laying on of hands from the prophet Samuel and becomes the next king of Israel.

1 Samuel 16:7-13 KJV

"But the Lord said unto Samuel, 'Look not on his countenance, or on the height of his stature; because I have refused him: for the Lord seeth not as man seeth; for man looketh on the outward appearance, but the Lord looketh on the heart.'

Then Jesse called Abinadab, and made him pass before Samuel. And he said, 'Neither hath the Lord chosen this.'

Then Jesse made Shammah to pass by. And he said, 'Neither hath the Lord chosen this.'

Again, Jesse made seven of his sons to pass before Samuel. And Samuel said unto Jesse, 'The Lord hath not chosen these.'

And Samuel said unto Jesse, 'Are here all thy children?' And he said, 'There remaineth yet the youngest, and, behold, he keepeth the sheep.' And Samuel said unto Jesse, 'Send and fetch him: for we will not sit down till he come hither.'

And he sent, and brought him in. Now he was ruddy, and withal of a beautiful countenance, and goodly to look to. And the Lord said, 'Arise, anoint him: for this is he.'

Then Samuel took the horn of oil, and anointed him in the midst of his brethren: and the Spirit of the Lord came upon David from that day forward. So, Samuel rose up, and went to Ramah."

Power Point 21

Design of the Prophetic Gift

"The prophetic was never designed to be about your image, however the purity of it is strengthened and developed through intimacy with the Father."

The closer you stay to the heart of the Father, the more you guard your heart against impurity. There are so many things that will attempt to compete for your time, affection, attention, and your assignment.

Your image is not as important as your intimacy with the Lord. Now I'm not excusing you to dress inappropriately, but use godly wisdom when it comes to your image. Because at the end of the day, it's more important to stand before God and please him than to please man.

1 Timothy 1:5 KJV

"Now the end of the commandment is charity out of a pure heart, and of a good conscience, and of faith unfeigned…"

1 Timothy 4:12 KJV

"Let no man despise thy youth; but be thou an example of the believers, in word, in conversation, in charity, in spirit, in faith, in purity."

D. John Coleman

"When prophets get into the vein of God, personality or popularity will not move them away from that intimate and pure place."

Power Point 22

The Prophetic Balance

"Prophetic balance will protect you from prophetic disorder."

Proverbs 11:1 KJV

*"A false **balance** is abomination to the Lord: but a just weight is his delight."*

Proverbs 20:23 KJV

*"Divers weights are an abomination unto the Lord; and a false **balance** is not good."*

1 Corinthians 14:40 AMP

"But all things must be done appropriately and in an orderly manner."

It is so easy these days for prophetic ministry gifts to be off. Balance in the prophetic has to be desired and pursued. It's something as a gift that you want to have. There are so many prophetic ministry gifts that have their lives not running parallel with what they teach and declare. This is why it is so important for those of us who are seasoned in the Word and have some type of prophetic stability, to be able to pour back into this generation and prophetic gifts. Let's look at how the Apostle Paul mentored and poured into several others and the benefits there.

These men that allowed themselves to be balanced were blessed and increased in their gifts.

One of the sad things that I often see is that some prophetic gifts really believe they're okay where they are, and that's not really the case. We need people in our lives to challenge us, not always compliment us.

This is the kind of culture we've built where right is wrong, and wrong is right. No one wants to address or deal with prophetic gifts that are off. This has never been the intent of God for prophetic gifts to stay or be in the dark concerning their prophetic gifts. Sometimes you may be off, or you may need to pray more or study your Word more and be okay with that. One of the main deterrents I've noticed for prophetic ministry gifts getting balanced is that one word which at the end of the day causes man to sin—that word called *pride*.

It can destroy a ministry gift as quickly as it rises.

Power Point 23

Motivation and Manipulation

"When it comes to the word of knowledge and the spirit of prophecy, if love is not the motivation, then it's manipulation."

Love is something we much learn how to demonstrate when it comes to the prophetic ministry. Love is what makes an impact, it makes a connection with the person whom you are ministering to. Jesus was a prime example of love in action. Love is not a word you just say, but it's also an action.

1 Corinthians 13:1 KJV

> *"Though I speak with the tongues of men and of angels, and have not charity, I am become as sounding brass, or a tinkling cymbal."*

Prophets, I strongly want to caution you to make sure you're grounded in the Word of God. Because this gift is often misused, and certain people will back away from it, particularly churches that are not familiar with the spirit of prophecy. Let's just for a moment review the two words here:

Manipulation: control or influence (a person or situation) cleverly, unfairly, or unscrupulously.

Synonyms: exploit, control, influence, use/turn to one's advantage, maneuver, engineer, steer, direct, guide, twist round one's little finger, work, orchestrate, choreograph

Manufacture: invent or fabricate (evidence or a story).
"the tabloid industry that manufactures epochal discoveries out of thin air"

Synonyms: make up, invent, fabricate, concoct, hatch, dream up, think up, trump up, devise, formulate, frame, contrive, construct, coin;

Power Point 24

The Environment of the Prophet

"Prophets, your place is not in Endor with the profits! It's in Eden where the real prophets dwell. Prophets are driven by His presence; profits are driven by their performance! The environment you submit to is critical to your maturity and development as a prophet."

Endor was a place in the tenure of King Saul of Israel. It was a place where they banned the mediums and witches. What we may address or recognize as divination or magic.

1 Samuel 28:3-7 KJV

"Now Samuel was dead, and all Israel had lamented him, and buried him in Ramah, even in his own city. And Saul had put away those that had familiar spirits, and the wizards, out of the land.

And the Philistines gathered themselves together and came and pitched in Shunem: and Saul gathered all Israel together, and they pitched in Gilboa.

And when Saul saw the host of the Philistines, he was afraid, and his heart greatly trembled.

> *And when Saul enquired of the Lord, the Lord answered him not, neither by dreams, nor by Urim, nor by prophets.*
>
> *Then said Saul unto his servants, 'Seek me a woman that hath a familiar spirit, that I may go to her, and enquire of her.' And his servants said to him, 'Behold, there is a woman that hath a familiar spirit at Endor.'"*

As prophets, we must know that our environments can determine our atmospheres. Being in the right place as a prophet is critical. Hanging in the wrong camp, tribe, or community can be very harmful to your spiritual man on the inside.

I have learned respectfully over the years to revere and honor my set place. What you tend to honor, respect will increase and stay in your life; but what you don't will exit.

Let's look at Eden, a place or disposition that was created because of communion with God. Eden is that type of place where there's fellowship with God. It's that kind of place where I believe as prophets, we increase in humility and we stay in that place. I have also personally discovered that this place called Eden is symbolic to worship. When prophetic ministry gifts practice daily, creating an environment for God to live in, then we can encounter the supernatural on the as a regular occurrence.

Endor will not be on your radar because of the reality of who God is to you. However, if you don't know Him for yourself, then you are subject to become something that was never intended by God for you to become—a profit!

Endor was that place were divinations, sorcery, and witchcraft resided. It was about the profit and not the people. This of course was during the tenure of Israel's first king, Saul. I strongly believe we all can learn from this and guard ourselves from a place called Endor. Endor is that open door to error and which will cause you to exit from the truth found in God's Word. Stay in your set place, prophets, before the Lord, and He will establish you!

Power Point 25

Strong Traits of a Prophet

"Prophets are not always conversational; they are often confrontational. They don't compromise, and they are Christ-natured with character, not competitive with other people's assignments."

What is the role of a prophet? *It's in the Bible*:

Deuteronomy 18:18-19, NKJV

> *"I will raise up for them a Prophet like you from among their brethren, and will put My words in His mouth, and He shall speak to them all that I command Him. And it shall be that whoever will not hear My words, which He speaks in My name, I will require it of him."*

God speaks to us through the prophets. *It's in the Bible*:

Hosea 12:10, NKJV

> *"I have also spoken by the prophets and have multiplied visions; I have given symbols through the witness of the prophets."*

God reveals His plans to the prophets. *It's in the Bible:*

Amos 3:7, NKJV

> *"Surely the Lord God does nothing, unless He reveals His secret to His servants the prophets"*

It's to our benefit to listen to God's prophets. *It's in the Bible:*

2 Chronicles 20:20, NKJV

> *"…Hear me, O Judah and you inhabitants of Jerusalem: Believe in the Lord your God, and you shall be established; believe His prophets, and you shall prosper."*

How does God speak to His prophets? *It's in the Bible:*

Numbers 12:6, NKJV

> *"Hear now My words: If there is a prophet among you, I, the Lord, make Myself known to him in a vision; I speak to him in a dream"*

Why did God send prophets? To guide his people in the right way. *It's in the Bible:*

2 Chronicles 24:19, NKJV

> *"Yet He sent prophets to them, to bring them back to the Lord; and they testified against them, but they would not listen."*

Traits of Prophets

Prophets are climate changers.
Prophets are agents of change.

Prophets are priests and sons and daughters, not bastards, nomads, and gypsies! WE DON'T NEED ANY MORE NOMAD PROPHETS! (Nomads: members of a community of people who live in different locations, moving from one place to another.)

Prophets are atmosphere adjusters.

Prophets are revelation releasers.

Prophets are servers of God's people, not servers of self.

Prophets are principality destroyers.

Prophets are not settlers but seekers.

Prophets are kingdom-minded not empire-driven.

Prophets are sensitive not ambitious.

Prophets are authoritative.

Prophets don't release generic prophecies, but specific ones!

Power Point 26

DOD: Discernment, Order, and Discipline

"Discernment, Order and Discipline (DOD) distinguishes the difference between a prophet and a profit."

Matthew 7:15-20 KJV

> *"Beware of false prophets, which come to you in sheep's clothing, but inwardly they are ravening wolves.*
>
> *Ye shall know them by their fruits. Do men gather grapes of thorns, or figs of thistles?*
>
> *Even so every good tree bringeth forth good fruit; but a corrupt tree bringeth forth evil fruit.*
>
> *A good tree cannot bring forth evil fruit, neither can a corrupt tree bring forth good fruit.*
>
> *Every tree that bringeth not forth good fruit is hewn down and cast into the fire.*
>
> *Wherefore by their fruits ye shall know them."*

Now, on the other hand, when it comes to the authentic prophet, they're under the authority of heaven and not man.

They walk or beat at the drum of the Spirit of the Lord.

Prophets are not necessarily popular. *It's in the Bible:*

Matthew 5:11-12, NKJV

> *"Blessed are you when they revile and persecute you and say all kinds of evil against you falsely for My sake. Rejoice and be exceedingly glad, for great is your reward in heaven, for so they persecuted the prophets who were before you."*

Prophets are not popular, because they speak what is right, not what is popular. *It's in the Bible:*

Isaiah 30:10, NIV

> *"They say to the seers, 'See no more visions!' and to the prophets, 'Give us no more visions of what is right! Tell us pleasant things, prophesy illusions.'"*

How can we recognize a true prophet? Their predictions will occur as predicted. *It's in the Bible:*

Jeremiah 28:9, NKJV

> *"As for the prophet who prophesies of peace, when the word of the prophet comes to pass, the prophet will be known as one whom the Lord has truly sent."*

I hope that covers for you what a prophet is versus a profit.

Power Point 27

Public and Private Interpretations

"All private interpretation in reference to the prophetic should not be made public especially when there's a lack of its true understanding."

Exodus 31:3 KJV

*"And I have filled him with the spirit of God, in wisdom, and in **understanding**, and in knowledge, and in all manner of workmanship..."*

2 Peter 1:19-21 KJV

"We have also a more sure word of prophecy; whereunto ye do well that ye take heed, as unto a light that shineth in a dark place, until the day dawn, and the day star arise in your hearts:

Knowing this first, that no prophecy of the Scripture is of any private interpretation.

For the prophecy came not in old time by the will of man: but holy men of God spake as they were moved by the Holy Ghost."

As prophetic ministry gifts, we must not allow ourselves to open a door or erroneous teaching and revelations. This is often how several ministry gifts get off in life and abort their assignments. I know some of you reading this right now can attest to someone you know or perhaps know of who got completely off.

This is why we need to be trained and equipped consistently on the subject of the prophetic ministry. So many people have these revelations but cannot back it up with the Scriptures. Personally, to the best of my ability—whether I'm preaching in a meeting or teaching something on social media—I make it my business to point out certain Scripture references. This really does help those of us who are very strong in the prophetic. Staying on the mark so that you won't miss it by error is imperative to your development as a prophetic ministry gift.

You are chartering very dangerous territory when you become closed-minded, shut people out, or isolate yourself from others because you feel they are not on your level.

Some prophets have opened doors that they have lost themselves behind, and they find it hard to return back. A biblical perspective of this would be to look at the characteristics of a reprobate mind. I have personally known of individuals who once were sold out for the things of God, only to lose touch or sight of their purpose and derail from the path of the Lord. I certainly believe there are not just ministry gifts that are impacted by this, but Christians in general. They get lost in their own ideologies and interpretations of serving the Lord and will make every attempt to try and justify their actions. Just as sin is sin, so is error the same as error. You're either hot or cold—there is no lukewarm or in between.

Revelations 3:14-16 KJV

> *"He that hath an ear, let him hear what the Spirit saith unto the churches.*
>
> *And unto the angel of the church of the Laodiceans write; These things saith the Amen, the faithful and true witness, the beginning of the creation of God;*

> *I know thy works, that thou art neither cold nor hot: I would thou wert cold or hot.*
>
> *So then because thou art lukewarm, and neither cold nor hot, I will spue thee out of my mouth."*

We have to entertain the things of the Spirit of God and not allow the influence of outside things.

There should be ample time invested privately in getting to know the Scriptures. We shouldn't, as prophetic gifts, test it on people in the public, especially when it has not been weighed out by the Word.

As prophetic ministry gifts, when it comes to interpretations, it is so important to have them measured by the Holy Spirit. The Holy Spirit will never steer or lead you into darkness. The Spirit of God illuminates and causes light to dispel the darkness so that there is clarity and understanding.

Wisdom should always be applied when it comes to the things of the Lord. We even practice this principle in the natural as well. There is no way over, around, or through wisdom. The Bible refers to wisdom as *her*. She will guide and lead you to your destination in the things of God—if you allow her to lead you.

Proverbs 2:1-8 KJV

> *"My son, if thou wilt receive my words, and hide my commandments with thee;*
>
> *So that thou incline thine ear unto wisdom, and apply thine heart to understanding;*
>
> *Yea, if thou criest after knowledge, and liftest up thy voice for understanding;*
>
> *If thou seekest her as silver, and searchest for her as for hid treasures;*
>
> *Then shalt thou understand the fear of the Lord and find the knowledge of God.*

> *For the Lord giveth wisdom: out of his mouth cometh knowledge and understanding.*
>
> *He layeth up sound wisdom for the righteous: he is a buckler to them that walk uprightly.*
>
> *He keepeth the paths of judgment, and preserveth the way of his saints."*

Now it has come to my attention that there is a bit of an epidemic as it relates to the misunderstanding and misinterpreting the words of the Lord. Almost to the degree that many people are losing their minds to miscalculating the things they have appeared to have received from the Lord. Some people had literally slipped into a mode of, *it's my life and I'll do it how I see fit.* When in reality, you don't have that luxury of messing up the lives of others—including yourself! You were bought with a price, which was the Precious Blood of Jesus.

Unfortunately, in our churches, many ministry gifts have succumbed to a reprobate mind. At one time, they were on fire; and somewhere along the way, something occurred that perverted their perspectives and they lost focus. People that I've known personally in ministry have begun to live as the world does; their respect for God is not twisted by their own perceptions now. It's like some of them can't see the wrong or don't choose to see the right anymore. It hurts my heart when I see this occur, as I'm quite sure it may grieve the heart of God. So many people depend on the ministry gifts that they often struggle with the pressure of compromise or they even quit the ministry. So many leaders are here in this place of struggle or have already transitioned in their relationships with God. But there's hope because God is a restorer, if you want to be restored. Praise God!

I pray right now if you're in that place of struggle currently in your life, that the love of God overshadows and overwhelm you in such a way that would be undeniable and also strengthening, in Jesus' Name.

When it comes down to the mind, God created it for a purpose: to comprehend and relate, to be able to process a thought or thing, and even to be able to function with all your faculties.

The mind is man's moral judgment. It is that faculty of man by which he is able to distinguish between good and evil. It is that faculty of man by which he can distinguish between the truth and the lie, between righteousness and unrighteousness. Not only does the mind distinguishes, but it is also that faculty that counsels the will. We might say that the mind is our moral attorney. It tells us what we should do and what we should not do. This is one of the main functions of the mind.

Let's look at this statement of a reprobate mind for a moment, because I believe, quite a few believers hang around this place in life. We see often that people say or do what they want these days anyhow. Our mind is such a precious commodity that if the enemy can win it over, he's won. This is why renewing our mind, washing our mind, and allowing our mind to meditate on the Word can be very beneficial to us giving the Word as to those that will be receiving it.

Now what's so surprising to me is that I did a research on how many books were written on the subject relative to the Christian faith on a reprobate mind, only to discover there were not that many. There are so many Christians who are trapped in this state of mind that it can't continue to be ignored or overlooked. The Church is not just spiritually sick, but naturally sick as well. Outside of spiritual deliverance, there's also a need to be mentally stable. In other words, the balancing of the two can accomplish much for the Kingdom of God.

Romans 1:28 KJV

> "And even as they did not like to retain God in their knowledge, God gave them over to a reprobate mind, to do those things which are not convenient…"

If you have any knowledge about courts, you have probably heard about Probate Court. *Probate* means *a court process by which a will is proved valid or invalid.* There could be any number of other legal issues involved too, but primarily, a probate is to prove the authenticity or fallacy of a will. It is a legal determination, so to have a *"reprobate mind"* means *to have no authenticity or to be in an invalid relationship with God, and particularly with Jesus Christ.*

Reprobation, in Christian theology, is a doctrine of the Bible found in many passages of Scripture, including, among others, **Romans 1:20-28, Proverbs 1:23-33, John 12:37-41**, and **Hebrews 6:4-8**, which teaches that a person can reject the gospel to a point where God in turn rejects them and curses their conscience to do unnatural and abominable things. When a sinner has become so hardened that they feel no remorse or misgiving of conscience, it is considered a sign of reprobation. This isn't teaching that because of their wicked actions that God will not save them, but it *is* teaching that God has withdrawn His offer of salvation and He gives them over to a seared conscience and now they can do vile actions. The vile actions and the many different things are evidence of a reprobate mind.

The English word, *reprobate*, is from the Latin root *probare* (*English*: prove, test), and thus derived from the Latin, *reprobatus* (reproved, condemned), the opposite of *approbatus* (commended, approved).

The Greek word of reprobate *is adokimos*, (which denotes the word *rejected*). **(Jeremiah 6:30)**

Let's look at several signs of a reprobate mind. I pray this provides clarity on this subject.

1) The Scriptures of God no longer convict you.
2) Your own conscience no longer convicts you when you do wrong. (You have become numb to the things that concern God.)
3) You start losing the ability to discern right from wrong.
4) You start calling "good" evil and "evil" good.
5) You have ignored the voice of God so long that the Holy Spirit is on mute in your life.
6) The Word of God is no longer the final authority in your life. It has lost its value in your life. You do what you feel is right instead of what God's Word says is right.

7) You start to believe a lie as the truth, and you walk in strong deception.
8) You start making excuses for the way you are.
9) The desire to please God is no longer there. You only strive to do those things that please yourself.
10) You get nauseated at the taste of sound doctrine. You cannot stomach truth, so you prefer fables.
11) You are uncorrectable; you see anyone who challenges you to grow in the things of God as an enemy.
12) You have "itching-ear syndrome,"—you want to hear only those things that tickle the flesh and emotions.
13) You have established your own righteousness. In your own eyes, you're okay. You have become blind to your own shortcomings which offend God. You measure yourself by the failure of others instead of by the Word of God.
14) Even if you do see and recognize these signs in your life, you don't care. You have an "Oh Well" attitude about life, and there is no sense of urgency to change.

Now, let me touch on two important components of the teaching and preaching ministry:

1. *Exegesis:* "to lead out of"
   This is the exposition, extraction, and explanation of a text. It is concerned with discovering the true meaning of the text, respecting its grammar, syntax, and setting.
2. *Eisegesis:* "to lead into"
   This is the reading of one's own ideas into Scripture. It means it is focused on making a point, perhaps even at the expense of the meaning of words.

We must be very cautious that we do not *always* approach Scriptures from a point of *Eisegesis*. When we do this, we can open the door to erroneous doctrine. The Word is where we should always start and end. Perhaps as prophets and prophetic gifts, we should approach the prophetic more from the perspective of *exegesis* ("to lead out of.")

In other words, standing on the Word or building on the Word will take us further than having an assumption of what a text means. Nobody in their right mind will go out on the water unless they know they have the adequate support that they need to hold them above water. When we have the Word with the prophetic, it will keep us above the water!

I want to charge you as prophetic ministry gifts to always be open to what you may hear God is saying, and always be open to confirmation and counsel concerning that Word.

Power Point 28

Prophetic Words Are Not Always Final

"Prophetic words are not always final; there must be a company of others who are sensitive and established in the prophetic to judge it or weight it out."

1 Corinthians 14:24-33 KJV

"But if all prophesy, and there come in one that believeth not, or one unlearned, he is convinced of all, he is judged of all:

And thus, are the secrets of his heart made manifest; and so, falling down on his face he will worship God, and report that God is in you of a truth.

How is it then, brethren? when ye come together, every one of you hath a psalm, hath a doctrine, hath a tongue, hath a revelation, hath an interpretation. Let all things be done unto edifying.

If any man speak in an unknown tongue, let it be by two, or at the most by three, and that by course; and let one interpret.

> *But if there be no interpreter, let him keep silence in the church; and let him speak to himself, and to God.*
>
> *Let the prophets speak two or three and let the other judge.*
>
> *If anything, be revealed to another that sitteth by, let the first hold his peace.*
>
> *For ye may all prophesy one by one, that all may learn, and all may be comforted.*
>
> *And the spirits of the prophets are subject to the prophets.*
>
> *For God is not the author of confusion, but of peace, as in all churches of the saints."*

I believe that when it comes to the spirit of prophecy, we must keep in mind that just because it *sounds* like God and it *seems* like God, this doesn't necessarily mean that it *is* God. With the Holy Spirit comes the ability to discern and judge if it's legitimate or not. I say this often—*just because it's prophetic does not mean that it's relevant to you and your situation.* Just because you may have the title of a prophet, have your name on the door and travel here and there…*this does not validate your authenticity!"* You must learn to inspect what you expect! You can make the sound of a dog…but that doesn't *make you* a dog! I want to challenge you to increase your Word intake so you can recognize foolishness for what it is.

Of course, part of prophecy has to do with confirmation. This is when God may have spoken to you already on something particular and then it's confirmed out of the mouth of a prophetic ministry gift. There are so many prophetic words given all the time and there are many prophets or gifts sometimes in one setting. I have nothing against prophets, as I am one myself. However, when you have a service and everyone has a prophetic word, something is wrong here, I believe. It doesn't take God a long time to move or speak. He's already willing and able. He's just looking for an available vessel to speak through. You can judge a prophetic word by the Word, and by seasoned prophets and established leaders in that setting.

1 John 4:1 KJV

> *"Beloved, believe not every spirit, but try the spirits whether they are of God: because many false prophets are gone out into the world."*

Any supposed prophetic teaching that contradicts or conflicts with what God has previously revealed or stated demonstrates itself to be from another source. Thus, a prophetic utterance must first be in sync with what God has already revealed. The Bible says to be on guard against false prophecies.

Galatians 1:6-10 KJV

> *"I marvel that ye are so soon removed from him that called you into the grace of Christ unto another gospel:*
>
> *Which is not another; but there be some that trouble you and would pervert the gospel of Christ.*
>
> *But though we, or an angel from heaven, preach any other gospel unto you than that which we have preached unto you, let him be accursed.*
>
> *As we said before, so say I now again, if any man preaches any other gospel unto you than that ye have received, let him be accursed.*
>
> *For do I now persuade men, or God? or do I seek to please men? for if I yet pleased men, I should not be the servant of Christ."*

Prophecy or prophetic words should *always* reveal Jesus Christ.

People should never be pointed towards singing your praises.

Revelation 19:10 KJV

"And I fell at his feet to worship him. And he said unto me, 'See thou do it not: I am thy fellow servant, and of thy brethren that have the testimony of Jesus: worship God: for the testimony of Jesus is the spirit of prophecy.'"

There must be a track record of moral consistency in their lives when it comes to the spirit of prophecy. Also, as I stated earlier, allowing leaders to judge your prophetic words.

1 Thessalonians 5:20-23 KJV

"Despise not prophesying.

Prove all things; hold fast that which is good.

Abstain from all appearance of evil.

And the very God of peace sanctify you wholly; and I pray God your whole spirit and soul and body be preserved blameless unto the coming of our Lord Jesus Christ."

Power Point 29

Keys to Successful Prophetic Ministry

"One of the keys to a successful prophetic ministry is to consistently stay in the secret place."

Psalm 91:1 KJV

> *"He that dwelleth in the secret place of the most High shall abide under the shadow of the Almighty."*

This is very important to consider. If you're called to the office of a prophet, it will require you to sacrifice your life until He has the audience of your heart. Prophets, we have such a job to do and to be effective in it, we must learn His heart. How do I learn His heart, you may ask? Getting in the Scriptures daily, studying them regularly, and meditating on them.

Joshua 1:7-8 KJV

> *"Only be thou strong and very courageous, that thou mayest observe to do according to all the law, which Moses my servant commanded thee: turn not from it to the right hand or to the left, that thou mayest prosper withersoever thou goest.*

> *This book of the law shall not depart out of thy mouth; but thou shalt meditate therein day and night, that thou mayest observe to do according to all that is written therein: for then thou shalt make thy way prosperous, and then thou shalt have good success."*

Daniels 2:29 KJV

> *"As for thee, O king, thy thoughts came into thy mind upon thy bed, what should come to pass hereafter: and he that revealeth **secrets** maketh known to thee what shall come to pass."*

God so desires to share His secrets with His people. As much as some people desire to really hear from heaven, God desires that much more. He desires to commune with us on a daily basis.

Amos 3:7 KJV

> *"Surely the Lord God will do nothing, but he revealeth his secret unto his servants the prophets."*

With everything going on in our world today in the government, and even in the Church, there has to be a venue for God to speak to us. For this same and very good reason does He raise up prophetic voices who have their ears constantly next to the mouth of God. As I often say, God is always speaking…we are just not always in the right place to hear Him.

To be able to have a strong prophetic gift that allows you to restore or resolve a current crisis in someone's life is simply amazing. So many people in the world today are looking for answers. The implication here is that there are things that are hidden and concealed that need to be highlighted.

The prophet Jeremiah declares, *"Call unto me; search me out!"*

Jeremiah 33:1-3 KJV

"Moreover, the Word of the Lord came unto Jeremiah the second time, while he was yet shut up in the court of the prison, saying,

'Thus, saith the Lord the maker thereof, the Lord that formed it, to establish it; the Lord is his name;

Call unto me, and I will answer thee, and show thee great and mighty things, which thou knowest not.'"

Power Point 30

Prophetic Gifts Type

"A good indicator of what type of prophetic gift you are can be determined by what kind of fruit that hits the ground as a result of your life."

Genesis 9:7 KJV

> *"And you, be ye **fruitful**, and multiply; bring forth abundantly in the earth, and multiply therein."*

John 15:1-8 KJV

> *"I am the true vine, and my Father is the husbandman.*
>
> *Every branch in me that beareth not fruit he taketh away: and every branch that beareth fruit, he purgeth it, that it may bring forth more fruit.*
>
> *Now ye are clean through the word which I have spoken unto you.*
>
> *Abide in me, and I in you. As the branch cannot bear fruit of itself, except it abide in the vine; no more can ye, except ye abide in me.*

I am the vine, ye are the branches: He that abideth in me, and I in him, the same bringeth forth much fruit: for without me ye can do nothing.

If a man abides not in me, he is cast forth as a branch, and is withered; and men gather them, and cast them into the fire, and they are burned.

If ye abide in me, and my words abide in you, ye shall ask what ye will, and it shall be done unto you.

Herein is my Father glorified, that ye bear much fruit; so, shall ye be my disciples."

Luke 6:43-45 KJV

"For a good tree bringeth not forth corrupt fruit; neither doth a corrupt tree bring forth good fruit.

For every tree is known by his own fruit. For of thorns men do not gather figs, nor of a bramble bush gather they grapes.

A good man out of the good treasure of his heart bringeth forth that which is good; and an evil man out of the evil treasure of his heart bringeth forth that which is evil: for of the abundance of the heart his mouth speaketh."

Power Point 31

Self-made Prophets

"Beware of self-appointed, homemade, and overnight prophets! Moses, Elijah, Elisha, Isaiah, Daniel, and so on—they were not made overnight! Prophets are processed daily and over a lifetime."

For every prophet that is reading this right now, please know that prophets are not made overnight…in a week…in a month…in a year…not even in *five* years. It is a making that stretches out over a lifetime.

God is the only originator of setting the prophets in office. There are those who are self-appointed, but God is and always will be the author and the architect.

1 Corinthians 12:28 KJV

> *"And God hath set some in the church, first apostles, secondarily prophets, thirdly teachers, after that miracles, then gifts of healings, helps, governments, diversities of tongues."*

Power Point 32

The Importance of Foundation

"Foundation has not been emphasized enough in the prophetic and the result of this product is damaged goods, fruity, and flaky prophetic gifts and dysfunctional degenerates! We are a culture that chases after prophetic ministry instead of prophetic maturity! Lord, your gifts need balance; it's the only real way to build your prophetic gift."

Isaiah 28:16 KJV

> *"Therefore, thus saith the Lord God, 'Behold, I lay in Zion for a **foundation** a stone, a tried stone, a precious corner stone, a sure **foundation**: he that believeth shall not make haste.'"*

Prophets, there is no way around foundation. Jesus was a prime example of four things: a foundation stone, a tried stone, a precious cornerstone, and a sure foundation.

What are you standing on, Prophet?

Remember, in **Matthew 7:24-27**, Jesus paints for us a great example of a house being built upon the sand or a solid foundation in:

Matthew 7:24-27 AMP

THE TWO FOUNDATIONS

"So everyone who hears these words of Mine and acts on them, will be like a wise man [a far-sighted, practical, and sensible man] who built his house on the rock. And the rain fell, and the floods and torrents came, and the winds blew and slammed against that house; yet it did not fall, because it had been founded on the rock. And everyone who hears these words of Mine and does not do them, will be like a foolish (stupid) man who built his house on the sand. And the rain fell, and the floods and torrents came, and the winds blew and slammed against that house; and it fell—and great and complete was its fall."

It is so imperative that as prophetic ministry gifts, we allow the Holy Spirit to create in us the appetite, passion, and heart for foundation, as it relates to our prophetic gifts. So much of what we currently see in the Church today is either off or has only half truth to it.

As a prophetic generation, we must continue to glean from the prophets of old.

God desires for our gifts to mature and prosper, but in the right manner. So, let's model ourselves after our great mentor and example—Jesus, the Son of God.

Zechariah 8:9 KJV

"Thus, saith the Lord of hosts; 'Let your hands be strong, ye that hear in these days these words by the mouth of the prophets, which were in the day that the foundation of the house of the Lord of hosts was laid, that the temple might be built.'"

Foundation and structure are vital when it comes to the prophetic. People are far out there or gone into the prophetic ministry, but they never really take the adequate time to become proficient. This is a place where we often miss the mark. Prophetic proficiency is absolutely necessary when it comes to being productive in this area of gifting.

> It is a sad truth that some people just don't get it…or just don't *care* to get it. You can't have or build *anything* unless there is first a solid foundation.

A solid foundation implies that I make the appropriate investments concerning the area of my gifting. A solid foundation takes time; it requires patience and wisdom.

So many prophetic gifts just don't spend the time necessary to perfect their giftings.

Through biblical contexts, we learn for instance that a prophet is one who speaks for God, expressing His will and purpose in words and signs. The office of a prophet is to forth-tell God's purpose through His Law and tell people God's Word.

> The prophet that ministers in the spirit of prophecy serves a two-fold purpose: to *foretell* and to *forthtell*. *Forthtelling* is prescriptive. It speaks the truth of God's Word, not for the future but for today.
>
> *Foretelling* is predictive; it describes something that will happen in the future. Both of these are capable of edifying, exhorting, and comforting the Body of Christ.

A true prophet, never losing sight of the law of God, deals with local situations, events of the Messiah, events of the future, and events that are dual in application. The prophet described as "coming from outside the system" (who brings new truth building it upon the foundation of old truth) is contrasted with the priest who "conserves old truth" (given to them by a prophet).

A prophet goads people to urgently commit themselves to a righteous course of action, forcing them to make clear and often painful choices. Elijah and John the Baptist clearly fulfilled the role of a prophet. This word *goad* here means "*to provoke or annoy someone so as to stimulate some action or reaction.*"

For example, the prophet Ezekiel in Chapter 41, states the specifics in the building process. The facts are plain: you can't just throw something together. We see this so often in the Church. We all can learn as we pattern ourselves after the Bible and the examples before us all. Tragedy in the prophetic doesn't have to continue, let's learn, get up, and keep it moving.

This lengthy Scripture offers a thorough understanding of the attention to building and the details on what the prophet Ezekiel describes.

Ezekiel 41:1-26 KJV

> *"Afterward he brought me to the temple, and measured the posts, six cubits broad on the one side, and six cubits broad on the other side, which was the breadth of the tabernacle.*
>
> *And the breadth of the door was ten cubits; and the sides of the door were five cubits on the one side, and five cubits on the other side: and he measured the length thereof, forty cubits: and the breadth, twenty cubits.*
>
> *Then went he inward, and measured the post of the door, two cubits; and the door, six cubits; and the breadth of the door, seven cubits.*

So, he measured the length thereof, twenty cubits; and the breadth, twenty cubits, before the temple: and he said unto me, this is the most holy place.

After he measured the wall of the house, six cubits; and the breadth of every side chamber, four cubits, round about the house on every side.

And the side chambers were three, one over another, and thirty in order; and they entered into the wall which was of the house for the side chambers round about, that they might have hold, but they had not hold in the wall of the house.

And there was an enlarging, and a winding about still upward to the side chambers: for the winding about of the house went still upward round about the house: therefore, the breadth of the house was still upward, and so increased from the lowest chamber to the highest by the midst.

I saw also the height of the house round about: the foundations of the side chambers were a full reed of six great cubits.

The thickness of the wall, which was for the side chamber without, was five cubits: and that which was left was the place of the side chambers that were within.

And between the chambers was the wideness of twenty cubits round about the house on every side.

And the doors of the side chambers were toward the place that was left, one door toward the north, and another door toward the south: and the breadth of the place that was left was five cubits round about.

Now the building that was before the separate place at the end toward the west was seventy cubits broad; and the wall of the building was five cubits thick round about, and the length thereof ninety cubits.

So, he measured the house, a hundred cubits long; and the separate place, and the building, with the walls thereof, an hundred cubits long;

Also, the breadth of the face of the house, and of the separate place toward the east, a hundred cubits.

And he measured the length of the building over against the separate place which was behind it, and the galleries thereof on the one side and on the other side, a hundred cubits, with the inner temple, and the porches of the court;

The door posts, and the narrow windows, and the galleries round about on their three stories, over against the door, sealed with wood round about, and from the ground up to the windows, and the windows were covered;

To that above the door, even unto the inner house, and without, and by all the wall round about within and without, by measure.

And it was made with cherubim and palm trees, so that a palm tree was between a cherub and a cherub; and every cherub had two faces;

So that the face of a man was toward the palm tree on the one side, and the face of a young lion toward the palm tree on the other side: it was made through all the house round about.

From the ground unto above the door were cherubim and palm trees made, and on the wall of the temple.

The posts of the temple were squared, and the face of the sanctuary; the appearance of the one as the appearance of the other.

The altar of wood was three cubits high, and the length thereof two cubits; and the corners thereof, and the length thereof, and the walls thereof, were of wood: and he said unto me, 'This is the table that is before the Lord.'

And the temple and the sanctuary had two doors.

And the doors had two leaves apiece, two turning leaves; two leaves for the one door, and two leaves for the other door.

And there were made on them, on the doors of the temple, cherubim and palm trees, like as were made upon the walls; and there were thick planks upon the face of the porch without.

And there were narrow windows and palm trees on the one side and on the other side, on the sides of the porch, and upon the side chambers of the house, and thick planks."

Power Point 33

Thriving on the Wrong Things Can Be Dangerous

"Prophets nowadays have missed the concept of edify, exhort, and comfort. Some have evolved to Profits and left the wisdom of God's Prophet. They thrive off of popularity instead of His presence. Stop making people dependent on your gift, because it doesn't necessary mean you have a relationship with God. Prophets, your place is not Endor, it's Eden."

Romans 14:19 AMP

> *"So then, let us pursue [with enthusiasm] the things which make for peace and the building up of one another [things which lead to spiritual growth]."*

1 Thessalonians 5:11 AMP

> *"Therefore, encourage and comfort one another and build up one another, just as you are doing."*

As prophets of the Lord, we must contend for the faith and the integrity of the prophetic. We have a mandate and a mission to extend the Word of the Lord to a people.

Before you put something together, it is necessary to read the instructions. We live in a culture where time is not something that has been taken into consideration. There are a lot of people who operate in the prophetic gifts, but just don't take the time to invest in their gift. Your gift will be as strong as what you invest in it to maintain it.

When we don't spend the adequate time to study, we are subject to evolving into something that was not the original intent. As prophets and prophetic ministry gifts, we cannot allow the opinions, the popularity, and the accolades of men to sway us in the wrong direction. We must remain consistent and faithful in the things of the Spirit if we are to avoid the pitfalls that lay around to ensnare or trap us. Remember; as prophets, the only dependency there should be is when you, as the prophetic gift, depend constantly on the Lord, not the people who are depending on you. Continue to allow prophetic counsel to stay around you to keep you focused and faithful, and you'll stay humble, pure, and on track.

2 Timothy 2:1-7 AMP

> *"So, you, my son, be strong [constantly strengthened] and empowered in the grace that is [to be found only] in Christ Jesus. The things [the doctrine, the precepts, the admonitions, the sum of my ministry] which you have heard me teach in the presence of many witnesses, entrust [as a treasure] to reliable and faithful men who will also be capable and qualified to teach others. Take with me your share of hardship [passing through the difficulties which you are called to endure], like a good soldier of Christ Jesus. No soldier in active service gets entangled in the [ordinary business] affairs of civilian life; [he avoids them] so that he may please the one who enlisted him to serve. And if anyone competes as an athlete [in competitive games], he is not crowned [with the wreath of victory] unless he competes according to the rules. The hard-working farmer [who labors to produce crops] ought to be the first to receive his share of the crops. Think over the things I am saying [grasp their application], for the Lord will grant you insight and understanding in everything."*

Power Point 34

The Prophet, the Logos, and the Rhema Word

"As a prophet of God, I must build up on the Logos or the Word of God, then I can release the Rhema! Rhema is produced by a revelation of His word, not yours."

I am an advocate for education and information, but in addition to these two things, there is a need to be open to the possibility of being well-rounded or balanced by having the understanding of the *Logos* and be willing to go beyond it as the Spirit of God leads. As prophetic gifts, I believe that it is important for us to be very familiar with our area of gifting or expertise. I believe we should be familiar with the prophets of the old as well as the present, because if you don't understand the past, how can you look towards a bright future?

Information is not always a bad thing…*if it's balanced out.* There are so many prophetic ministry gifts that have very little word base or foundation. I don't believe that we should just assume God is going to help us in this department if we're not giving Him anything to work with.

In school, I was not always diligent in my studies; and now, in hindsight, I wish I had taken advantage of those moments. However, we all learn from our missed opportunities. School started off very challenging to me, particularly because I was dyslexic and was not aggressive in my studies. My parents had an education which went only through grammar school and a bit of high school, so they were very limited in their ability to help me. But over time, God gradually began to awaken in me a desire to want a better life, to be a better person, and to have a better attitude. Of course, I knew it wasn't just going to happen automatically. Over time, my appetite for reading and educating myself had changed considerably.

I am so grateful to God for not quitting on me when I almost quit on myself.

Let's bring a little of clarity to the words *Logos* and *Rhema*. I know these are two of the words that we throw around in our Christian language and sometimes lose sight of their meaning.

Logos is defined as: *"The Word of God, or principle of divine reason and creative order, identified in the Gospel of John with the second person of the Trinity incarnate in Jesus Christ."*

According to Vine's Expository Dictionary, the word translated as *Logos* in the Greek denotes *the expression of thought, embodying a conception or idea.*

According to the Venerable Strong's Concordance (#G4487), *Rhema* means *an utterance (individually, collectively, or specifically) on a particular matter or topic.*

Thayer's Greek Definitions defines the word as *something that has been uttered, in either the past or the present, by a living entity.*

Now in Greek: *that which is spoken, what is uttered in speech or writing; an utterance (individually, collectively, or specifically); the word by which something is commanded, directed, or enjoined; something that is spoken clearly and vividly, in unmistakable terms and in an undeniable language.* In the New Testament, the word *Rhema* carries the idea of *a quickened word.*

When we reference this word *Rhema* whether in conversation or demonstration, the *Logos*, which is the written word, has stood the test of time and has always provided the platform for us to venture into the prophetic realm or what we refer to as Rhema.

The word *Venerable* which is mentioned in this Strong's Concordance reference literally denotes according to the dictionary, *commanding respect because of great age or impressive dignity.*

Prophets, you don't have to go out and demand respect or anything relative to that. Just become the prophet the Lord has called you to be and do it unapologetically, and people that have a heart for God will honor you and respect you because of the *Logos* present in your life.

The first time *Rhema* is used in the New Testament is during Jesus' forty-day temptation by Satan. Jesus, after fasting for a long period and being tempted to feed himself through a miracle, responds with the following:

> *"But He (Jesus) answered and said, 'It is written, 'Man shall not live by bread alone, but by every word (Rhema) that proceeds out of the mouth of God.'"* **(Matthew 4:4, HBFV)**

Interestingly, the word *Rhema* occurs at least seventy times in the New Testament Greek text. The books that use it the most are the Gospel of Luke (19 times), followed by the Book of Acts (14 times), then the Gospel of John (12 times). In the King James Bible, the Greek word *Rhema* is many times translated as "word(s)" (**Matthew 4:4, 18:16, Mark 14:72**). It is also translated as "saying(s)" (**Mark 9:32, Luke 1:65**) and "thing" (**Luke 2:15, Acts 5:32**).

The second appearance of the word in the New Testament occurs in **Matthew 12**, when some self-righteous religious leaders accused the Lord of casting out demons by the power of Satan himself. He warns them that God will hold humans accountable for every idle (lazy, useless) word (*Rhema*) that is spoken (see **Matthew 12:24, 36**).

These two Greek words here in this section, *Logos* and *Rhema*, are two distinctions which I believe as prophetic gifts we should be able to distinguish.

Logos is the written word; while *Rhema*, is a spoken word.

As prophets, we hold the responsibility of carrying the Word of the Lord and we should not be biased or partial in our delivery. If God speaks a word, we must learn to yield, lean in, and trust the process of delivery. Sometimes, the delivery can be difficult, especially if it's someone you're familiar with. This is why I believe it's so important to have the Word in your heart and spirit. When the Word is present, it pushes you, challenges you, and assures you that you can do this.

If we let people get to us, we may be subject to twisting or changing a direct word. The written Word of God is our elevator that lifts us to the place where we are supposed to be as God's prophets and prophetic gifts.

As prophets, we can be very emotional or moody at times, but the Word should always bring us back or prevent us from going too far.

Prophets are human and we must, as the Body of Christ, never forget this! We are subject to fail at times and divert away from the Word. The Word is and will always be the guidepost and compass for every prophetic ministry gift.

Sometimes, we struggle with fear and insecurities, just as the prophet Elijah did. Operating in the office of a prophet is not all glitter and gold. Let me be one of the first to inform you, there will be moments of what I called the "Juniper Tree Experience."

"Side Effects of the Prophet"

- You may become susceptive to deception and divination if you're not discipled correctly.
- You will often encounter irregular or unexplainable mood swings.
- You will sometimes deal with rejection and isolation that no one else could possibly imagine.
- Your anointing may increase, but at great cost.
- You will often deal with an unusual dimension of witchcraft.
- You will, at times, experience mental attacks.
- You will be accused often as a false prophet for the scriptural perspective, position, and stance you take for your assignment.

Power Point 35

No Freelancing in the Prophetic

"The prophetic ministry does not include or involve freelancing."

According to Dictionary.com, the word *freelancing* is defined as *"Working for different companies at different times rather than being permanently employed by one company."*

The current state of the Church is that we actually have some prophetic gifts who get involved in going where there is more money or popularity involved. I remember years ago, someone mentioned to me how they would raise offerings. I thought to myself, *"That sounds like deception."* I had to immediately cast down and separate from that situation. The prophetic gift is something that should be treated as very precious and special.

I believe that in the prophetic ministry, we should have a mind that is certain and absolute—no time for games, tricks, and gimmicks. When you research the Scriptures, you will discover track records of prophets in the Old Testament and New Testament that were not unstable. They were permanently fixed in what the Lord had said.

For example, let's look at the prophet **Habakkuk** in Chapter 2:

Habakkuk 2:1-3 AMP

> *"I will stand at my guard post*
>
> *And station myself on the tower;*

And I will keep watch to see what He will say to me,

And what answer I will give [as His spokesman] when I am reproved.

Then the Lord answered me and said,

'Write the vision

And engrave it plainly on [clay] tablets

So that the one who reads it will run.

For the vision is yet for the appointed [future] time

It hurries toward the goal [of fulfillment]; it will not fail.

Even though it delays, wait [patiently] for it,

Because it will certainly come; it will not delay.'"

This should be a great example for us as prophetic ministry gifts to shadow and mirror.

Power Point 36

Truth Will Hold You Accountable if You Let It

"Truth will hold you accountable if you submit to it and hold you to the right course of prophetic order and you will increase in discipline, discernment, development, and demonstration as it relates to the prophetic ministry."

Deuteronomy 5:20 AMP

> *"You shall not give false testimony [that is, lie, withhold, or manipulate the **truth**] against your neighbor (any person)."*

Deuteronomy 6:7 AMP

> *"You shall teach them diligently to your children [impressing God's precepts on their minds and penetrating their hearts with His truths] and shall speak of them when you sit in your house and when you walk on the road and when you lie down and when you get up."*

Psalm 60:4 AMP

*"You have set up a banner for those who fear You [with awe-inspired reverence and submissive wonder—a banner to shield them from attack], A banner that may be displayed because of the **truth**. Selah."*

Truth is often a word in many people's vocabulary that's hard to practice at times. It's that word that will either expose you or enlarge you. On the other end of truth is always honor and reward which also involves sacrifice. As prophetic ministry gifts, we need to understand that the truth has to serve as the guidepost that directs our prophetic gifts. Because what truth will do is challenge you to stay straight when so many others have gone astray. Do not fall into the trap of keeping up with the Joneses or measuring yourself by others; the Scriptures admonish us of this.

2 Corinthians 10:12 KJV

"For we dare not make ourselves of the number or compare ourselves with some that commend themselves: but they measuring themselves by themselves, and comparing themselves among themselves, are not wise."

There is such a strong need for prophetic truth when it comes to operating in this particular assignment. There's a statement that I often say: *"Time will always reveal the extension of truth in an individual."*

Jeremiah 23:16 AMP

"Thus, says the Lord of hosts, "Do not listen to the words of the [false] prophets who prophesy to you. They are teaching you worthless things and are leading you into futility; They speak a vision of their

own mind and imagination and not [truth] from the mouth of the Lord."

John 16:13 KJV

"Howbeit when he, the Spirit of truth, is come, he will guide you into all truth: for he shall not speak of himself; but whatsoever he shall hear, that shall he speak: and he will shew you things to come."

Power Point 37

The Danger of Divination

"Divination is inspired by the demonic with the intent to deceive and disconnect you from an authentic encounter of God's demonstration in the prophetic!"

Divination: *"the art or practice that seeks to foresee or foretell future events or discover hidden knowledge usually by the interpretation of omens or by the aid of supernatural powers. Unusual insight; intuitive perception."*

The design of divination is to start subtle, with the intent to pull you away from the Spirit of truth and the Word of God.

> The Bible declares that it's the "small fox" that destroys the vine...the devil isn't coming with a red suit with horns on his head, a pitchfork in hand, and a long tail. He will come in the form of things and people close to you. Things you get fulfillment out of, such as friends, jobs, and business.

Remember that prophets point you towards God, and psychics divert your attention away from the things of God. Real prophets should always be in compliance with and always directing you to Christ and His plans for your life.

Divination serves to replace your dependence on the true and living God with the intent also to convince you that there is another way.

John 14:6 KJV

"Jesus saith unto him, 'I am the way, the truth, and the life: no man cometh unto the Father, but by me.'"

This spirit will try to compensate or replicate that which is the Spirit of God by any means necessary. It wants to have the governing realm over your spirituality. Unfortunately, ministry gifts fail here in this place and it can be the norm until they become immune to walking the wrong path.

Demons are real—there is demonic activity that opposes the Holy Spirit. This is why as prophetic ministry, we must arm ourselves continuously with truth. If you don't arm yourself with His truth, you become open to error, and you may become susceptible to developing a blind spot in the prophetic. Things like the truth can be right up on you, and you'll miss it, which could potentially cause a wreck in someone's life.

Power Point 38

Truth or Error, It's Your Choice

"When there's truth, there's prophetic power; where there is error, there is an open door to the spirit of divination."

John 8:32 KJV

> *"And ye shall know the truth, and the truth shall make you free."*

John 14:6 KJV

> *"Jesus saith unto him, 'I am the way, the truth, and the life: no man cometh unto the Father, but by me.'"*

Acts 1:8 KJV

> *"But ye shall receive power, after that the Holy Ghost is come upon you: and ye shall be witnesses unto me both in Jerusalem, and in all Judaea, and in Samaria, and unto the uttermost part of the earth."*

When prophetic gifts, particularly prophets, stay or walk in a place of power, movement of the miraculous is always imminent. They experience a dimension of God that's made available only through purity, passion, pursuit, and patience.

Psalm 37:34 KJV

"Wait on the Lord, and keep his way, and he shall exalt thee to inherit the land: when the wicked are cut off, thou shalt see it."

Isaiah 40:31 KJV

*"But they that wait upon the Lord shall **renew** their strength; they shall mount up with wings as eagles; they shall run, and not be weary; and they shall walk, and not faint."*

Power Point 39

Self-Gratification vs. Service-Edification

"Often when there's an increase of error, it's because prophets spend more time in a place called self-gratification than they do in a place called service and edification."

Gratification is defined as *"pleasure, especially when gained from the satisfaction of a desire."* Synonyms: *satisfaction, fulfillment, indulgence, relief, quenching.*

1 John 2:15-17 KJV

> *"Love not the world, neither the things that are in the world. If any man loves the world, the love of the Father is not in him.*
>
> *For all that is in the world, the lust of the flesh, and the lust of the eyes, and the pride of life, is not of the Father, but is of the world.*
>
> *And the world passeth away, and the lust thereof: but he that doeth the will of God abideth forever."*

There are several things I must note here. For starters, *no one* is exempt from sin. As long as you have a body with flesh on it, at some point, it will attempt to lead your life. This is why, as prophets, we must be very attentive to what voices we allow to have access to our lives. There's a saying that goes, *"You will be led through life by your dominant thoughts."*

Here in this text, John gives us three temptations that are of the world. Every adult human in history has been tempted with the lust of the flesh, the lust of the eyes, and the pride of life. From even great men such as Moses, Samson, and King David.

It is important to be aware of these three areas of temptation that we will all face. For every sin we commit, will be preceded by at least one of these temptations.

As a prophetic ministry gift, keep in mind that if you want to be kept, if you want to be holy, if you want to be pure, and if you want to be sold out for Him, just fight the good fight of faith because as a real believer, you always win in the end.

1 Corinthians 10:13 KJV

> *"There hath no temptation taken you but such as is common to man: but God is faithful, who will not suffer you to be tempted above that ye are able; but will with the temptation also make a way to escape, that ye may be able to bear it."*

Edification: *the instruction or improvement of a person morally or intellectually.*

Synonyms: *education, instruction, tuition, teaching, schooling, pedagogy, andragogy, tutoring, coaching, training, tutelage, guidance, enlightenment, cultivation, development, information, inculcation, indoctrination, improvement, bettering, uplifting, elevation.*

Romans 15:2 KJV

> *"Let every one of us please his neighbor for his good to edification."*

1 Corinthians 14:3 KJV

But he that prophesieth speaketh unto men to edification, and exhortation, and comfort.

2 Corinthians 13:10 KJV

"Therefore, I write these things being absent, lest being present I should use sharpness, according to the power which the Lord hath given me to edification, and not to destruction."

The Bible is full of men and women of God who did such a great job of edifying and building others up. Such as Abraham, Elijah and Elisha, Joshua and Caleb, and of course, the Apostle Paul, and Jesus' disciples.

Power Point 40

The Nature of the Prophetic Is Clarity Not Confusion

"The nature and character of the prophetic is clarity, not confusion!"

Paul, during his tenure, really put an emphasis on finding comfort as a believer. There were three things he discussed: to edify, to exhort, and lastly, to comfort. I believe as a child of God, you can have a significant degree of clarity that comes through comfort. When your mind is at peace or at ease, you process things more clearly, you hear better, and you move with patience and not frenzy.

To be Christ-like when it comes to the prophetic is very essential. Christ always demonstrated character, grace, and wisdom, and as a result, the anointing always increased. Prophets and prophetic gifts, if you want your anointing to increase, it won't happen by osmosis.

The prophetic gifting is not for sorcery, witchcraft, or any such thing. It's not for the purpose of people hearing how accurate or loud you are. The prophetic gift should always give you a sense or clarity and direction. If every time you get a prophetic word, you leave more confused than when you came, you might want to weigh the words before you accept them—it is your right! You don't have to accept everyone's prophetic word! Yes, I said it, and I will continue to do so.

Just as it is the nature of the fish to swim in the water, just as it is the nature of the birds to fly in the air, and just as it is human nature to breathe and inhabit the land, so is it with the prophetic ministry: to edify, exhort, and comfort!

There is definitely a specific nature to the prophetic. Prophecy flows as the Spirit of God wills it, not as you do.

Its nature is to make an impact on the world and unscramble the channels of a man's heart that have been receiving interference by the devil. To help get them on track or perhaps back on track for those who may have gone astray.

> Prophetic ministry gifts, take note. Do not put too much emphasis on a certain style. You cannot confine or restrict the Spirit of God to a certain genre or administration. Everyone has a different style…and *that's okay*! Always focus on what matters in the prophetic; understanding the operation and function of it.

Nothing is more crucial in a prophecy than the actual content of the prophecy. **We should always concentrate on prophetic content first—prophetic style second.** If style is important in a prophecy (which it is), then even more important is content.

Power Point 41

Beware of False Prophets

"The teaching of a false prophet cannot withstand the correction, challenge, and the nature of Christ through the light of His word."

In the realm of religion, a ***false prophet*** is *"one who falsely claims the gift of prophecy or divine inspiration, or to speak for God, or who makes such claims for evil ends."*

False prophets and false teachers are those who arrogantly attempt to fashion new interpretations of the Scriptures to demonstrate that these sacred texts should not be read as God's words to His children but merely as the utterances of uninspired men, limited by their own prejudices and cultural biases. They argue, therefore, that the Scriptures require new interpretation and that they are uniquely qualified to offer that interpretation.

When we think of false prophets and false teachers, we tend to think of those who espouse an obviously false doctrine or presume to have authority to teach the true gospel of Christ according to their own interpretation. However, I reiterate there are false prophets and false teachers who have or at least claim to have membership in the church. There are those who, without authority or consent, often from other ministries, claim church endorsement to their products and practices. Beware of such!

Jude 1:3-4 AMP

> "Beloved, while I was making every effort to write you about our common salvation, I was compelled to write to you [urgently] appealing that you fight strenuously for [the defense of] the faith which was once for all handed down to the saints [the faith that is the sum of Christian belief that was given verbally to believers]. For certain people have crept in unnoticed [just as if they were sneaking in by a side door]. They are ungodly persons whose condemnation was predicted long ago, for they distort the grace of our God into decadence and immoral freedom [viewing it as an opportunity to do whatever they want], and deny and disown our only Master and Lord, Jesus Christ."

According to this text here, the implication is that false teachers or prophets will come in secretly or subtly and mix truth with a lie. This is something that we see too often in our churches. False prophets thrive in a gullible or undiscerning environment.

2 Timothy 4:1-5 KJV

> "I charge thee therefore before God, and the Lord Jesus Christ, who shall judge the quick and the dead at his appearing and his kingdom;
>
> Preach the word; be instant in season, out of season; reprove, rebuke, exhort with all long suffering and doctrine.
>
> For the time will come when they will not endure sound doctrine; but after their own lusts shall they heap to themselves teachers, having itching ears;
>
> And they shall turn away their ears from the truth and shall be turned unto fables.

> *But watch thou in all things, endure afflictions, do the work of an evangelist, make full proof of thy ministry."*

Jeremiah 14:14 KJV

> *"Then the Lord said unto me, 'The prophets prophesy lies in my name: I sent them not, neither have I commanded them, neither spake unto them: they prophesy unto you a false vision and divination, and a thing of nought, and the deceit of their heart.'"*

Matthew 7:15 KJV

> *"Beware of **false prophets,** which come to you in sheep's clothing, but inwardly they are ravening wolves."*

The Bible does not beat around the bush; there will be false prophets in the land. There is a perspective that I feel as though I need to share regarding what we consider a false prophet, and it is this: false prophets are *not necessarily those whose words don't come to pass*! You can't coin a person as a false prophet because prophetic words were given that didn't come to pass. Sometimes, people's faith is not in the place where it should be, or perhaps their life is so messed up that it's going to take a renewing of the mind to begin with.

So, to all you prophets who may deal with people saying that you're false prophets when you know you're not, don't sweat it! There are so many reasons why certain prophecies never come to pass. Prophecies not coming to pass does not always mean that a person is not a true prophet. It will take patience, practice, and thick skin to continue to prophesy. God has a people that will respond and "hearken unto the Word of the Lord" that you release. In order for prophecy to be beneficial, it must be received openly and in faith on both sides. On one side, God is speaking to the prophet; and on the other side, He is speaking to the recipient. I just felt like I needed to remind someone of this, because the church and its people will kill your gift if you let it. Many times, just being in the right location or environment helps prophets and the prophetic ministry. Don't throw in your towel because of religious folks and naysayers.

Prophecies coming to pass are contingent upon two things: your *faith* and your *obedience to the Word.*

When you actually think about it, there probably wouldn't be as many so-called "false prophets" as there are now if we didn't live in a culture of people ready and willing to believe anything and everything you tell them. It's just like with the spirit of Jezebel in a sense, whereas that spirit can't thrive in an environment except if an Ahab is present! It is important to note here that as a church culture, we have failed in some areas and given life to things that shouldn't have any precedence over the Body of Christ. We often struggle with things and situations because of doors we've opened up in various areas of our lives. You can literally give life or death to a thing. If you feed it, it will live; and if you starve it, it will eventually die. I believe we give too much power and play to things that are erroneous, unrelated to Christ.

Proverbs 15:4 KJV

"A wholesome tongue is a tree of life: but perverseness therein is a breach in the spirit."

Proverbs 17:20 KJV

"He that hath a froward heart findeth no good: and he that hath a perverse tongue falleth into mischief."

Proverbs 18:21 KJV

"Death and life are in the power of the tongue: and they that love it shall eat the fruit thereof."

Characteristics of a False Prophet:

- False prophets often **cannot relate** to being planted or submitted.
- False prophets **love the crowds** more than the presence of God.
- False prophets **live for the praises** instead of the pleasures of God.
- False prophets **preach the gospel of prosperity only with the motive for self-advancement**, regardless of others.
- False prophets are **often disguised as sheep** but are really wolves.
- False prophets are **more so led by *a* spirit and not *the* Spirit** of the Lord.
- False prophets can move in miracles, but they **are not mounted in the Word**, which implies that their sense of power is based on the sight of a miracle, not the source of it.
- False prophets **will lead you away from Jehovah** and cause you to develop dependency on them.
- False prophets prophesy things that **never really come to pass**.
- False prophets **love the things of the world** more than they love God and His **Word**.
- False prophets **refuse to call out sin** for what it is.
- False prophets **don't believe in a hell** or preach repentance.
- False prophets **believe that *they* are the way**, not Jesus.
- False prophets display **selfish and opportunistic behavior**.
- False prophets **don't feel the prophecies need judging**.
- False prophets **live in the realm of divination and deception**.
- False prophets **spend very little time in prayer and in the Word**; they know just enough to get over on people.
- False prophets **counsel with no one other than themselves**.
- False prophets present the image of light but **are really walking in darkness**.

- False prophets **develop their own style of perverted, mixed-up worship.**
- False prophets are often charismatic and good communicators but **are horrible at breaking down the Scriptures.**
- False prophets **dislike being disciplined, discipled, and rebuked.**
- False prophets are **fueled by pride, popularity, and politics.**
- False prophets **avoid other prophets and ministry gifts** that know the **Word.**
- False prophets' **sermons never match their service.**
- False prophets often **connect with weaker Christians to feel superior or more powerful.**
- False prophets **live for the moments to be worshipped.**
- False prophets **mix heresy with truth.**

Let me just leave you with this small thought to ponder. I have come to the conclusion that prophets flow and broadcast from the *revelation* channel while on the other hand, false prophets flow in a realm of familiarity on the *information* channel.

Matthew 6:19-21 KJV

> *"Lay not up for yourselves **treasures** upon earth, where moth and rust doth corrupt, and where thieves break through and steal: But lay up for yourselves **treasures** in heaven, where neither moth nor rust doth corrupt, and where thieves do not break through nor steal: For where your treasure is, there will your heart be also."*

1 John 4:1-3 KJV

> *"Beloved, believe not every spirit, but try the spirits whether they are of God: because many false prophets are gone out into the world.*

Hereby know ye the Spirit of God: Every spirit that confesseth that Jesus Christ is come in the flesh is of God:

And every spirit that confesseth not that Jesus Christ is come in the flesh is not of God: and this is that spirit of antichrist, whereof ye have heard that it should come; and even now already is it in the world."

> "**False prophets** *publicize* what they *plagiarize*. **Prophets** *publicize* what they've *practiced* and *heard in private*."

Power Point 42

Prophets Unpack Destinies

"True prophets help unpack destinies and assist in directing history by way of prophetic decrees and declarations."

In the religious sense, a **prophet** is *"An individual who is regarded as being in contact with a divine being and is said to speak on that entity's behalf, serving as an intermediary with humanity by delivering messages or teachings from the supernatural source to other people."*

Amos 3:7 AMP

> *"Surely the Lord God does nothing without revealing His secret plan [of the judgment to come] to His servants the prophets."*

In the life of a believer, over a span of time, things developed. Some good, some bad. However, as this often occurs, things have the proclivity to build up to the extent that people can lose sight of their purpose. For whatever reason, this can cause a delay in walking in their God-given assignment. However, I am a firm believer these days that every delay is always working in your favor.

The Body of Christ is full of people who are indecisive, uncertain, and even confused as to what they are supposed to be doing at this season in their lives.

Joel 3:14 AMP

"Multitudes, multitudes in the valley of decision (judgment)! For the day of the Lord is near in the valley of decision [when judgment is executed]."

There can be possibly a series of events that may have happened in their lives that cause stagnation and procrastination. Please know that *the enemy doesn't want you to walk in your destiny.* There will be things from your past that will make every attempt to cause you to become dormant in the things of the Lord. I believe that somewhere in the subconscious mind, we can open up a door of defeat, depression, disappointment, despair, and discouragement. When this happens, a bridge is destroyed, and a block is established that permits you to only go so far. The bridge is destroyed, so now nothing exits, or nothing enters, and the block is established mentally, emotionally, spiritually, and financially. A lot of people get trapped in this state of living, when it was never the intention or plan of Jehovah God.

Ever wonder why you hear the expression, *"Every time I take one step forward, I take two steps back?"* It is a statement that sounds so familiar in the lives of many Christians—you can be an apostle, prophet, pastor, teacher, evangelist, minister, deacon, youth leader, or elder in a ministry. We all, to some degree, have some type of internal dilemma to contend with. I see this often in the Body of Christ where people feel so lost and need someone to assist them by giving direction.

This is why I'm so honored and privileged to be a part of the prophetic ministry. The prophetic ministry releases breath into some things that may have appeared to have been dead. The prophetic ministry gift releases that life that revives hopes and dreams. It confirms, aligns, and assigns you with who and where you're supposed to be. We need more authentic prophetic ministry gifts in our churches to release the captives in heart, mind, body, and soul.

Luke 4:18 AMP

> *"The Spirit of the Lord is upon Me (the Messiah), Because He has anointed Me to preach the good news to the poor. He has sent Me to announce release (pardon, forgiveness) to the captives, and recovery of sight to the blind, to set free those who are oppressed (downtrodden, bruised, crushed by tragedy)."*

This is why we need the five-fold ministry gifts to be strong, alert, and attentive to the things that are relative to God.

Matthew 23:34 AMP

> *"Therefore, take notice, I am sending you prophets and wise men [interpreters, teachers] and scribes [men educated in the Mosaic Law and the writings of the prophets]; some of them you will kill and even crucify, and some you will flog in your synagogues, and pursue and persecute from city to city."*

Ephesians 4:11 AMP

> *"And [His gifts to the church were varied and] He Himself appointed some as apostles [special messengers, representatives], some as prophets [who speak a new message from God to the people], some as evangelists [who spread the good news of salvation], and some as pastors and teachers [to shepherd and guide and instruct]."*

Power Point 43

Signs Don't Always Validate Authenticity

"When it comes to the office of the Prophet, signs and accuracy don't always equate to authenticity."

God has and will always speak through the mouth of His prophets. Of course, we know there are many other ways that God communicates with His people.

God reveals His will to humans:

- Through messages He gives to His prophets by direct communication, visions, or dreams delivered by angels.
- Through direct signs and miracles.
- Through His written Word, the Holy Scriptures, and the Bible.
- Through the influence of the Holy Spirit on the individual's Christian mind and heart.

Authentic has to do with *"That which has not been tainted, watered down, infused with a religious spirit, mixed with flesh and spirit, or infected by man's desire and will."*

> *Authentic prophets carry the mind and heart of God concerning matters relative to His Will.*

The word *authentic* always requires more, whether it be produced or if it's the original name brand of something. No one who has invested their time, energy, and money wants to acquire a knock-off version of an original.

When it comes to the prophetic ministry, I'm sure a lot of us have seen or witnessed "knock-off prophets" or "boot-leg versions" of a prophet. The Church unfortunately is full of them. They have made no prophetic investment in maturing their gifts; they are for the most part, just takers.

But I declare, God is raising up Thoroughbreds in the prophetic that will flow in purity in the prophetic ministry.

As prophets, we are inspired by the Holy Spirit, just as it were with those who wrote the Scriptures. They were all inspired. **(2 Timothy 3:16-17)**

The phrase "by inspiration of God" comes from the Greek word *Theopneustos*, meaning "God-breathed."

God's inspired writings give spiritual light, illumination, clarity, and guidance to mankind.

Matthew 7:21-23 AMP

> *"Not everyone who says to Me, 'Lord, Lord,' will enter the kingdom of heaven, but only he who does the will of My Father who is in heaven. Many will say to Me on that day [when I judge them], 'Lord, Lord, have we not prophesied in Your name, and driven out demons in Your name, and done many miracles in Your name?' And then I will declare to them publicly, 'I never knew you; depart from Me [you are banished from My presence], you who act wickedly [disregarding My commands].'"*

2 Peter 2:1-3 AMP

> *"But [in those days] false prophets arose among the people, just as there will be false teachers among you, who will subtly introduce destructive heresies, even denying the Master who bought them, bringing swift destruction on themselves. Many will follow their shameful ways, and because of them, the way of truth will be maligned. And in their greed, they will exploit you with false arguments and twisted doctrine. Their sentence [of condemnation which God has decreed] from a time long ago is not idle [but is still in force], and their destruction and deepening misery is not asleep [but is on its way]."*

Being able to prophesy or flow in the prophetic does not confirm you as a prophet, just as flowing in the working of miracles doesn't either.

Power Point 44

The Prophet's Nature

"The nature of the prophet is to flow in the spirit; the nature of a profit is to flow in the flesh."

Romans 8:14 NIV

> *"For those who are led by the Spirit of God are the children of God."*

Prophets that understand their purpose and assignment develop the nature of a prophet. The nature of the prophet is simple: being open and sensitive to the timing and the voice of the Lord concerning His Church. This is a lifestyle that is congruent to that of the prophets of old and even that of Jesus the Son of God. The nature that should be the most visible is that of love. The nature of a real prophet doesn't lust to get ahead at any cost. Instead, they are compassionate when they need to be and confrontational when they need to be. Prophets flow in the realm of the Spirit of God.

Revelations 2:7 AMP

> *"He who has an ear, let him hear and heed what the Spirit says to the churches. To him who overcomes [the world through believing that Jesus is the Son of*

> *God], I will grant [the privilege] to eat [the fruit] from the tree of life, which is in the Paradise of God.'"*

Profits on the other hand, flow in an opposite direction. Their nature is to satisfy the soul as opposed to the Spirit of God.

Proverbs 14:12 NIV

> *"There is a way that appears to be right, but in the end, it leads to death."*

Proverbs 21:2 AMP

> *"Every man's way is right in his own eyes, But the Lord weighs and examines the hearts [of people and their motives]."*

Power Point 45

The Prophet's Spiritual Diet

"Prophets have a specific diet! Worship, praying, fasting, becoming more familiar with the Word, and following the wind of God."

John 4:23-24 AMP

> *"But a time is coming and is already here when the true worshipers will worship the Father in spirit [from the heart, the inner self] and in truth; for the Father seeks such people to be His worshipers. God is spirit [the Source of life, yet invisible to mankind], and those who worship Him must worship in spirit and truth."*

Real prophets are always attracted to the heart of worship. The prophetic and worship work hand in hand together. Prophets begin to flow in a greater anointing when there is an atmosphere of worship. You cannot be a mature prophet of God and exclude worship out of your regimen.

2 Kings 3:15 AMP

> *"'But now bring me a musician.' And it came about while the musician played, that the hand (power) of the Lord came upon Elisha."*

We see here in this text that the anointing came mighty upon the prophet and he begin to prophesy.

Deuteronomy 8:3 AMP

> *"He humbled you and allowed you to be hungry and fed you with manna, [a substance] which you did not know, nor did your fathers know, so that He might make you understand [by personal experience] that man does not live by bread alone, but man lives by every word that proceeds out of the mouth of the Lord."*

Matthew 5:6 AMP

> *"Blessed [joyful, nourished by God's goodness] are those who hunger and thirst for righteousness [those who actively seek right standing with God], for they will be [completely] satisfied."*

Prophets have a distinct appetite for the things of God. The desire to hear His voice drives them to constantly pursue Him. Prophets have a longing for the tangible presence of God and to see miracles happen in the lives of the people of God. Prophets require times of isolation for the purpose of focusing on His voice. Satisfying the flesh is not a part of their regular regimen. They have a regimen in place that requires them to be in sync and in tune with God's heartbeat.

John 4:13-14 AMP

> *"Jesus answered her, 'Everyone who drinks this water will be thirsty again. But whoever drinks the water that I give him will never be thirsty again. But the water that I give him will become in him a spring of water [satisfying his thirst for God] welling up [continually flowing, bubbling within him] to eternal life.'"*

> You cannot expect to be exceptional in your prophetic gift as a prophet if you don't do the appropriate things to increase that anointing.

It can be as simple as what I initially stated: praying, fasting, and giving yourself to the studying of the Word.

John 3:30 AMP

"He must increase [in prominence], but I must decrease."

Even though there is a prophetic grace on the prophets, we still have to do our part. The degree to which you invest in your gift determines your outcome or results. I know there are some that may lean on that grace, but there's such a greater dimension to experience in the prophetic—I call it the *optimum levels of overflow*. I could give you some Greek and Hebrew here, but I want this to be very elementary, so that a fifth grader could grab it and run.

I know a lot of people these days don't care to hear about praying and fasting! But Jesus emphasizes to his twelve disciples, to pray, fast, and give.

A lifestyle of prayer helps develop your spiritual muscles in the prophetic. It conditions you to settle down and hear His voice. Prayer can cause you to strengthen your ability to focus on the objectives at hand. When you look at every prophet from the Old Testament to the New Testament, you will discover they all had an active life of prayer! Being a prophet doesn't give you the grounds to stop praying because you think you've arrived. It's a trick of the devil to trip you up into a trap of complacent territory, a settling setback, and destroy your destiny. This is why we must be persistent in our push to pray.

Let's look at the significance of fasting. There is an acronym I want to share with you for the word *fast*.

Forward motion, accelerated, giving

Access into the supernatural,

Superimposing power of God, and unlocking a new

Territory.

Ezra 8:21-23 NKJV

"Then I proclaimed a fast there at the river of Ahava, that we might humble ourselves before our God, to seek from Him the right way for us and our little ones and all our possessions. For I was ashamed to request of the king an escort of soldiers and horsemen to help us against the enemy on the road, because we had spoken to the king, saying, "The hand of our God is upon all those for good who seek Him, but His power and His wrath are against all those who forsake Him." So, we fasted and entreated our God for this, and He answered our prayer."

Fasting is *"The willing abstinence or reduction from some or all food, drink, or both, for a period of time."* An absolute fast or dry **fasting** is normally defined as *"abstinence from all food and liquid for a defined period."* This is the dictionary's answer.

Let's look at a biblical definition of ***fasting***.

Biblical ***fasting*** can be defined as *"Abstaining from food, in some cases, certain liquids for a certain period of time for spiritual purposes which produce the results of becoming more receptive and open to God."*

Fasting is mentioned in Scriptures one third as much as prayer, or about seventy-five times.

The word fast in Hebrew is ***Tsum***, which means *"to cover the mouth."*

Fasting helps you reexamine your heart and find clarity for your assignment.

Fasting releases revelation and understanding about your vision, and the vision of the house.

> **"Christian fasting, at its root, is the hunger of a homesickness for God. Christian fasting is not only the spontaneous effect of superior satisfaction in God, it is also a chosen weapon against every force in the world that would take that satisfaction away."** ~John Piper

When we fast the right way as believers, several things can occur:

1. Fasting and prayer can help us **hear from God**.
2. Fasting and prayer can **reveal our hidden sins**.
3. Fasting and prayer can **strengthen intimacy with God**.
4. Fasting and prayer can **teach us to pray with the right motives**.
5. Fasting and prayer can **build our faith**.

I want to strongly encourage you to develop a lifestyle of fasting. There are so many benefits that are at your disposal as you posture yourself in this position of fasting and praying.

1. Fasting is an invitation (God does not punish you if you don't; you'll eventually punish yourself and keep the door of delay open).
2. Fasting is a grace: when you decide to step up and say, "I'm going to fast," instantly, the Holy Spirit begins to partner with you.
3. Fasting is humbling yourself.
4. Fasting is a form of worship.
5. Fasting is the *private discipline* that brings *public reward*.

Matthew 6:16-18 NIV

> *"When you fast, do not look somber as the hypocrites do, for they disfigure their faces to show others they*

are fasting. Truly I tell you, they have received their reward in full. But when you fast, put oil on your head and wash your face, so that it will not be obvious to others that you are fasting, but only to your Father, who is unseen; and your Father, who sees what is done in secret, will reward you.

Biblical figures who fasted and received great blessings:

- ***Jesus*** endured a 40-day fast before he began his earthly ministry (**Matthew 4:1-17**).
- ***Moses*** observed a 40-day fast, after which received the Ten Commandments (**Exodus 20:1-26**).
- ***Daniel*** endured a 21-day fast, during which he received the blessing of wisdom beyond that of anyone else in the empire (**Daniel 10**).
- ***Esther*** implored all the Jews in the city to observe a 3-day fast, during which she gained a favorable audience with the king who spared her people (the Jews) whom Haman wanted to annihilate (**Esther 3-8**).
- ***Hannah*** "wept and did not eat" because of her sorrow over infertility; after this fasting period, she conceived Samuel (**1 Samuel 1:1-11**).
- ***Paul*** was fasting when he received God's call and the assignment God had for his life (**Acts 9:7-9**).
- ***Peter*** was fasting when he received a new revelation and call to take the gospel to the Gentiles (**Acts 10**).
- ***Jehoshaphat*** endured a fast which allowed him to learn the Lord's plan on how to defeat an army (**2 Chronicles 20**).
- ***Elijah*** endured a fast and received a word from God that affected even the next generation (**I Kings 18-19**).
- ***Joseph*** spent time fasting while in prison and after his release, gained a highly respected position as second-hand man to the pharaoh of Egypt (**Gen. 41:39-45**).
- ***Solomon*** humbled himself in fasting and prayer and God greatly increased his wealth and wisdom (**Kings 3:10-13**).

Finally, let's look at applying ourselves as prophets by studying the Word of the Lord. It is so important as prophetic ministry gifts that we familiarize ourselves with the Scriptures. As prophets especially, let's be able to back up our prophetic words or insight by the barometer of the Word.

The study component cannot be overlooked or disregarded. As prophetic ministry gifts to the Church, we must be able to effectively communicate the Bible in such a way that we don't sound like a heretic, or like someone who has no clue what they are talking about. You get such a greater value out of the prophetic as you search the Scriptures and meditate on them.

Joshua 1:5-8 KJV

> *"There shall not any man be able to stand before thee all the days of thy life: as I was with Moses, so I will be with thee: I will not fail thee, nor forsake thee.*
>
> *Be strong and of a good courage: for unto this people shalt thou divide for an inheritance the land, which I sware unto their fathers to give them.*
>
> *Only be thou strong and very courageous, that thou mayest observe to do according to all the law, which Moses my servant commanded thee: turn not from it to the right hand or to the left, that thou mayest prosper withersoever thou goest.*
>
> *This book of the law shall not depart out of thy mouth; but thou shalt meditate therein day and night, that thou mayest observe to do according to all that is written therein: for then thou shalt make thy way prosperous, and then thou shalt have good success."*

As prophets, we learn that success is not automatic. It doesn't happen because you wish it—it has to be planned.

Here are some Scriptures for you to study:

Matthew 22:29 NIV

"Jesus replied, 'You are in error because you do not know the Scriptures or the power of God.'"

Acts 17:11 NIV

"Now the Berean Jews were of more noble character than those in Thessalonica, for they received the message with great eagerness and examined the Scriptures every day to see if what Paul said was true."

1 Timothy 4:13-14 NIV

"Until I come, devote yourself to the public reading of Scripture, to preaching and to teaching. Do not neglect your gift, which was given you through prophecy when the body of elders laid their hands on you."

2 Timothy 2:14 NIV

"Do your best to present yourself to God as one approved; a worker who does not need to be ashamed and who correctly handles the word of truth."

Power Point 46

The Prophet's Home Is Not the Platform, but His Presence

"The home of every prophet is not the platform; it should always be the presence of the Lord."

Psalm 16:11 AMP

"You will show me the path of life;

In Your presence is fullness of joy;

In Your right hand there are pleasures forevermore."

Word of wisdom: never let your motive be to stand up before the crowd. Never allow yourself as a prophet to get caught up in the fame, making a name, or playing the game. The platform should be for those who have sacrificed and put in the time and have proven themselves to be worthy of the honor of standing on the platform.

Make sure you do ministry the right way. As prophets of God, the more we want to seek His face, the less we desire to try and get in the face of the people.

The Bible is full of prophets who sought the things of the Lord. One of my favorites is the prophet Samuel, whom the Bible said, *"he turned his heart toward the things of the Lord; none of his words fell to the ground."*

Samuel had the **Scripture**. Samuel had **Stability**. Samuel had been **Submitted**. Samuel was **Sold out** for the Lord; and because he didn't seek the platform, he was not **Suspect**!

Power Point 47

The Watchman Prophet

"Prophets are not called to be only a voice, but also a watchman or spokesman in the spiritual and natural realm. They are to be extensions of God's plan in the earth, bridge builders to another people's purpose and destiny. They are to be multi-dimensional with the ability to equip and train."

Ezekiel 33:1-9 NIV

> *"The Word of the Lord came to me: 'Son of man, speak to your people and say to them: "When I bring the sword against a land, and the people of the land choose one of their men and make him their watchman, and he sees the sword coming against the land and blows the trumpet to warn the people, then if anyone hears the trumpet but does not heed the warning and the sword comes and takes their life, their blood will be on their own head. Since they heard the sound of the trumpet but did not heed the warning, their blood will be on their own head. If they had heeded the warning, they would have saved themselves. But if the watchman sees the sword coming and does not blow the trumpet to warn the people and the sword comes and takes someone's life, that person's life will be taken because of their*

sin, but I will hold the watchman accountable for their blood.'

'Son of man, I have made you a watchman for the people of Israel; so, hear the word I speak and give them warning from me. When I say to the wicked, "You wicked person, you will surely die," and you do not speak out to dissuade them from their ways, that wicked person will die for their sin, and I will hold you accountable for their blood. But if you do warn the wicked person to turn from their ways and they do not do so, they will die for their sin, though you yourself will be saved."'

Power Point 48

Prophets Increase as They Stay Under the Mantle

"Prophets that stay under a mantle, which implies alignment, will attract unprecedented miracles and experience unparalleled momentum. They will walk in their respective assignments without confusion and disappointment."

Prophets are always to be *subject to* and *remain under* the leading of the Holy Spirit. One of the reasons I believe that prophets get out of order is because they lack an understanding of the mantle. It involves more than just a covering. The mantle has to do with the alignment component. It is relative to alignment just as the office of a prophet is relative to that of the assignment. There has been so much misinterpreting on this subject. When prophets understand their assignments, there is no need to feel insecure or inferior. You have the superior one living inside of you.

A *mantle*, according to the Merriam-Webster Dictionary, is *"a figurative cloak symbolizing preeminence or authority,"* or *"something that covers, enfolds, or envelops."* This can be interpreted from the external, or natural, perspective. However, I believe this is just one aspect of the mantle. There is also an internal or spiritual component as well, and this is the other aspect that I would like for you to consider, which is relative to leadership. When character is in place, it validates the calling and the assignment of the office.

The ***mantle*** is that which is initiated by God. It is the containment of the supernatural of a man or woman of God. It is the capacity to carry an anointing of authority in an office or position. It's the disposition. The covering or the mantle is revealed and released through a revelation of the Scriptures through fasting and prayer, and most importantly, discipline.

I don't think that the main struggle is with the *office* of the prophet; rather, I believe that it is with the *mantle*. So many prophets and prophetic gifts struggle with authority and accountability. There are attitudes and certain dispositions that people have that can be either helpful or harmful, both to others in the church and to themselves.

Prophets are human, and they too can struggle with flesh issues. Please note, they are not exempt from sin. The fact that they live in a human body is an indication that temptation can enter and knock on the heart at any given time. We are all susceptible to sin. There has to be a choice made daily as a ministry gift to do the right thing even as it relates to life in general. We live in a society where choices are made every day: Should I marry him/her? Should I go to college? Should I buy a new house or car? So many choices are presented to us all and most of us are intelligent enough to know that there's a wrong and a right choice to make. However, the choice to honor God with your gift is very significant to your longevity in ministry.

Now just for a moment, let's discuss this word *lust*. **Lust** is a spirit that if not checked, will pull you into a place or direction you may find it difficult to return from. It is that same spirit that infiltrated Lucifer and he was demoted as a result of it. He had the position, but somewhere in his mind or heart, he lost focus and there were consequences.

Isaiah 14:12-15 NKJV

"How you are fallen from heaven,

O Lucifer, son of the morning!

How you are cut down to the ground,

> *You who weakened the nations!*
>
> *For you have said in your heart:*
>
> *I will ascend into heaven,*
>
> *I will exalt my throne above the stars of God;*
>
> *I will also sit on the mount of the congregation*
>
> *On the farthest sides of the north;*
>
> *I will ascend above the heights of the clouds,*
>
> *I will be like the Most High.'*
>
> *Yet you shall be brought down to Sheol,*
>
> *To the lowest depths of the Pit."*

Let me share with you another acronym here for the word **lust**.

Losing direction due to the flesh,

Unction for sin or the desire of it,

Slave to satisfying self, and giving in to

Temptation.

Let me just state this for the record: **lust is not and will never be the substitute for love**. As prophets of the Lord, the mantle is the connection and covering that keeps us on course. We see this all the time in the prophetic ministry— prophets doing things that are unsanctioned or unauthorized. Because they are prophets, sometimes people ignore the sin or disorder. This is why we really need to distinguish the difference between the mantle and the office of the prophet. The Book of James validates this instance of how one can either be trapped or be free and prosper doing it God's way and not your own.

James 1:12-18 AMP

> "Blessed [happy, spiritually prosperous, favored by God] is the man who is steadfast under trial and perseveres when tempted; for when he has passed the test and been approved, he will receive the [victor's] crown of life which the Lord has promised to those who love Him. Let no one say when he is tempted, 'I am being tempted by God' [for temptation does not originate from God, but from our own flaws]; for God cannot be tempted by [what is] evil, and He Himself tempts no one. But each one is tempted when he is dragged away, enticed and baited [to commit sin] by his own [worldly] desire (lust, passion). Then when the illicit desire has conceived, it gives birth to sin; and when sin has run its course, it gives birth to death. Do not be misled, my beloved brothers and sisters. Every good thing given and every perfect gift is from above; it comes down from the Father of lights [the Creator and Sustainer of the heavens], in whom there is no variation [no rising or setting] or shadow cast by His turning [for He is perfect and never changes]. It was of His own will that He gave us birth [as His children] by the word of truth, so that we would be a kind of first fruits of His creatures [a prime example of what He created to be set apart to Himself—sanctified, made holy for His divine purposes]."

This is why we as prophets need the appropriate people in our lives to help us stay grounded and guided by the Holy Spirit and not Casper, the friendly ghost. We really need to always reference the story of the prophet Elijah and Elisha.

The assignment can be made clear in the life of a prophet, but it's what they often do when the reality of that office is active in their life. The assignment, as I have stated in my previous book, *Rising of the Thoroughbreds*, is relative to the office of the prophet.

So many prophets deliberate and struggle over the two. Notice that I stated here, the *two*. They are not the same. For so many years, prophets have not been equipped enough with the balance of their office. We slap titles on people too quickly and have not allowed them to be proven by the process.

Assignments are given out regularly throughout the Body of Christ; but unfortunately, not everyone complies or applies the principle of that position. I want to challenge you to stay under the mantle, which is alignment. You will get further in your gifting and build character continuously along the way. Walk in your place of grace, stay under the mantle, and don't pattern or measure your gifts by others that you see. Don't set yourself up to fail but choose to be successful.

Walk in your Metron and own it! Make the devil and every religious spirit regret they ever attacked your life.

"Walking under a mantle will always require the spirit of honor and humility for that grace to flow fluently in your life. Without it, you'll just hover around and not maximize your gift."

Power Point 49

Disconnecting from Self

"The only way the real prophets can speak is if they disconnect from self and connect to the Spirit of God and continue to have a heart of service for the Body of Christ."

Deuteronomy 6:4-7 KJV

> *"Hear, O Israel: The Lord our God is one Lord:*
>
> *And thou shalt love the Lord thy God with all thine heart, and with all thy soul, and with all thy might.*
>
> *And these words, which I command thee this day, shall be in thine heart."*

Matthew 22:37-40 KJV

> *"Jesus said unto him, Thou shalt love the Lord thy God with all thy heart, and with all thy soul, and with all thy mind. This is the first and great commandment. And the second is like unto it, Thou shalt love thy neighbor as thyself. On these two commandments hang all the law and the prophets."*

What we have discovered about prophets is that they must learn to be spiritually sound when it comes to flowing in the gift of prophecy.

We have a mandate as prophets to stay intimate with the Father, infused in His Word and influenced by the Holy Spirit. When this continues to occur on a regular basis, then and only then we will we be able to disconnect from things that try to monopolize our abilities. Disconnection regards relocation, refocusing, readjusting, realigning, and reconstructing your life.

Sometimes, God has to disconnect you to reconnect you. He knows better than you do—what is required and what will benefit you in the long run.

I want to encourage you: don't fight the process, allow the disconnecting of some current things in your life, and watch and see God take you to some places that you've only imaged.

"The highest order of a gifting is not a title, it's service. It's the voice that speaks and expresses louder than the mouth."

Power Point 50

Prophets Are Not Here to Accommodate

"As a prophet of God, I am not here to accommodate and make friends. I am here to infiltrate the enemy's plans, make an impact, influence others with truth, and always inquire the wisdom and knowledge from the Holy Spirit."

Prophets, *we don't have the luxury of being everyone's friend!* If they will trade *Jesus* for Barabbas, what do you think they will do for you? Jesus was once again the example of a great prophet—one who loved the people of God with no ulterior motive. He knew perhaps there would be some that reject him. But as a man sent by God on assignment, He kept on plowing. He influenced a culture and time with His teachings, His lifestyle, and the compassion He constantly displayed. It was never about competition, it was never about them serving Him only, it was never about His name being in lights. He wanted to do the will of the Father, and that was it.

A great story to reference here would be that of the prophet Jeremiah. He demonstrated compassion and love for the people, and it wasn't about popularity for him because he knew his assignment.

Jeremiah 1:4-10 NIV

"The Word of the Lord came to me, saying, 'Before I formed you in the womb, I knew you, before you

were born, I set you apart; I appointed you as a prophet to the nations.'

'Alas, Sovereign Lord,' I said, 'I do not know how to speak; I am too young.' But the Lord said to me, 'Do not say, "I am too young." You must go to everyone I send you to and say whatever I command you. Do not be afraid of them, for I am with you and will rescue you,' declares the Lord.

Then the Lord reached out his hand and touched my mouth and said to me, 'I have put my words in your mouth. See, today I appoint you over nations and kingdoms to uproot and tear down, to destroy and overthrow, to build and to plant.'"

"Prophets pursue and acquire the audience of heaven and things become activated and answered on earth as God's speaks through them."

Power Point 51

Diligence Is Required in the Prophetic Ministry

"There are two words that are often hidden in the word diligence as it relates to the prophetic ministry in Hebrew 11:6. They are the words "discipline" and "discernment." As prophetic gifts, we can never become proficient without the two."

Proverbs 8:17 NIV

"I love those who love me, and those who seek me find me."

Proverbs 12:24 NIV

"Diligent hands will rule, but laziness ends in forced labor."

Usually, when we think about diligence, we think about a good work ethic. Diligence should not be used only at the workplace. It should be used in all areas of our lives. Diligence in your walk of faith leads to greater spiritual growth, a greater love for others, greater love for Christ, and a greater understanding of the gospel and God's love for you. Where diligence *is*, procrastination and laziness *are not*. We must never slack while doing God's will.

> **"Let's be diligent in giving, careful in our living, and faithful in our praying." ~Jack Hyles**

Discipline: *"The practice of training people to obey rules or a code of behavior, using punishment to correct disobedience."*

Synonyms: *"control, regulation, direction, order, authority, rule, strictness, a firm hand."*

All of the following Scriptures are in the King James Version:

Hebrews 12:11

"Now no chastening for the present seemeth to be joyous, but grievous: nevertheless, afterward it yieldeth the peaceable fruit of righteousness unto them which are exercised thereby."

Proverbs 12:1

"Whoso loveth instruction loveth knowledge: but he that hateth reproof [is] brutish."

Proverbs 13:24

"He that spareth his rod hateth his son: but he that loveth him chasteneth him betimes."

1 Corinthians 9:27

"But I keep under my body and bring [it] into subjection: lest that by any means, when I have preached to others, I myself should be a castaway."

Hebrews 12:5-6

"And ye have forgotten the exhortation which speaketh unto you as unto children, My son, despise

not thou the chastening of the Lord, nor faint when thou art rebuked of him."

Proverbs 3:11-12

"My son, despise not the chastening of the LORD; neither be weary of his correction."

Revelation 3:19

"As many as I love, I rebuke and chasten: be zealous therefore, and repent."

Proverbs 23:13

"Withhold not correction from the child: for [if] thou beatest him with the rod, he shall not die."

Hebrews 12:5-11

"And ye have forgotten the exhortation which speaketh unto you as unto children, My son, despise not thou the chastening of the Lord, nor faint when thou art rebuked of him."

Proverbs 29:15

"The rod and reproof give wisdom: but a child left [to himself] bringeth his mother to shame."

Titus 1:8

"But a lover of hospitality, a lover of good men, sober, just, holy, temperate…"

Proverbs 20:13

"Love not sleep, lest thou come to poverty; open thine eyes, [and] thou shalt be satisfied with bread."

Proverbs 6:23

"For the commandment [is] a lamp; and the law [is] light; and reproofs of instruction [are] the way of life..."

Proverbs 29:17

"Correct thy son, and he shall give thee rest; yea, he shall give delight unto thy soul."

Proverbs 22:15

"Foolishness [is] bound in the heart of a child; [but] the rod of correction shall drive it far from him."

Proverbs 25:28

"He that [hath] no rule over his own spirit [is like] a city [that is] broken down, [and] without walls."

Hebrews 13:17

"Obey them that have the rule over you and submit yourselves: for they watch for your souls, as they that must give account, that they may do it with joy, and not with grief: for that [is] unprofitable for you."

Discernment: *"the ability to judge well."*
Synonyms: *"judgment, taste, discrimination, refinement, cultivation, sophistication, enlightenment, sensitivity, subtlety; insight, perceptiveness, perception, perspicacity; astuteness, acumen, shrewdness, ingeniousness, cleverness, intelligence, sharpness, wisdom, erudition, awareness, sagacity."*

The spiritual gift of discernment is also known as the gift of "discernment of spirits" or "distinguishing between spirits." The Greek word for the gift of discernment is *Diakrisis*.

The word describes being able to distinguish, discern, judge, or appraise a person, statement, situation, or environment. In the New Testament, it describes the ability to distinguish between spirits, as in **1 Corinthians 12:10**, and to discern good and evil as in **Hebrews 5**: See also **I Corinthians 12:10, Acts 5:3-6; 16:16-18; 1 John 4:1**.

Deuteronomy 32:38 AMP

*"They are a nation without sense, there is no **discernment** in them."*

1 Kings 3:7-14 NIV

"'Now, Lord my God, you have made your servant king in place of my father David. But I am only a little child and do not know how to carry out my duties. Your servant is here among the people you have chosen, a great people, too numerous to count or number. So, give your servant a discerning heart to govern your people and to distinguish between right and wrong. For who is able to govern this great people of yours?'

The Lord was pleased that Solomon had asked for this. So, God said to him, 'Since you have asked for this and not for long life or wealth for yourself, nor have asked for the death of your enemies but for discernment in administering justice, I will do what you have asked. I will give you a wise and discerning heart, so that there will never have been anyone like you, nor will there ever be. Moreover, I will give you what you have not asked for—both wealth and honor—so that in your lifetime you will have no equal among kings. And if you walk in obedience to me and keep my decrees and commands as David your father did, I will give you a long life.'"

Psalm 78:72 AMPC

*"So [David] was their shepherd with an upright heart; he guided them by the **discernment** and skillfulness [which controlled] his hands."*

Psalm 119:66 AMPC

*"Teach me good judgment, wise and right **discernment**, and knowledge, for I have believed (trusted, relied on, and clung to) Your commandments."*

Psalm 119:125 AMPC

*"I am Your servant; give me understanding (**discernment** and comprehension), that I may know (discern and be familiar with the character of) Your testimonies."*

Proverbs 4:1 AMPC

*"Hear, my sons, the instruction of a father, and pay attention in order to gain and to know intelligent **discernment**, comprehension, and interpretation [of spiritual matters]."*

Proverbs 4:7 AMPC

"The beginning of wisdom is: Get [skillful and godly] wisdom [it is preeminent]!

And with all your acquiring, get understanding [actively seek spiritual discernment, mature comprehension, and logical interpretation]."

Colossians 1:9 AMPC

*"For this reason, we also, from the day we heard of it, have not ceased to pray and make [special] request for you, [asking] that you may be filled with the full (deep and clear) knowledge of His will in all spiritual wisdom [in comprehensive insight into the ways and purposes of God] and in understanding and **discernment** of spiritual things."*

"Your ignorance is a weapon that can trap you and delay you, while knowledge can be a weapon to position you towards your assignment, purpose, and prosperity!"

Power Point 52

Prophetic Print

"Prophets have a distinct prophetic print, an unusual dimension of prophetic grace. They are able to touch all three administrations: the spirit of prophecy, the gift of prophecy, and the office of the prophet."

Ephesians 4:11-12 NIV

> *"So, Christ himself gave the apostles, the prophets, the evangelists, the pastors and teachers, to equip his people for works of service, so that the Body of Christ may be built up."*

Notice what the Apostle Paul was implying here in the text. I believe that when he mentioned "some" prophets, that's exactly what he meant. In other words, *all* are not prophets, but *some* are. However, we all can *desire* to prophesy.

Genesis 1:26-27 NIV

> *"Then God said, 'Let us make mankind in our image, in our likeness, so that they may rule over the fish in the sea and the birds in the sky, over the livestock and all the wild animals, and over all the creatures that move along the ground.'*

> *So, God created mankind in his own image, in the image of God he created them; male and female he created them."*

According to this text, God created us in *His* image, not the image of man. I want to point this out here! We all have been uniquely designed by God, even though we have the genetics of our natural parents. Now of course, they were used to assist you in getting here; but just like Jeremiah the prophet, we were chosen before they even knew us. This is so amazing how God created us in His image, and is still making and molding us daily. Whether we are five-fold gifts or not, we are all in the process of development.

All of us are here for a divine purpose. They may not all be the same, but the overall mandate is to advance the Body of Christ into their destinies.

For example, when you are born, the state requires a fingerprint and toeprint in most states to identify you. Well, that's how the natural works. No two thumbprints are alike in the natural. On the other hand, in the spirit, there's what I call a "prophetic thumbprint." I believe every prophetic ministry gift has one, and the same thing applies here—all prophetic ministry gifts have a specific prophetic print.

We all have been allotted a specified level of prophetic grace.

Think about this: there is only one Bishop Clarence E. McClendon, one T.D. Jakes, one Cindy Jacobs, one Dutch Sheets, one James Goll, one Jennifer LeClaire, one Rick Joyner, one Bill Johnson, one Mike Bickle, one John Eckhardt, and there is only one *you!* All of these ministry gifts have their own uniqueness that makes them special. Allow yourself the opportunity to discover yours.

When your prophetic print or identity is established, beware—lest you wake up and expose someone's real feelings towards you. Some of you know exactly what I am referencing. Some of you are in a season of "walking it out" at the risk of losing certain people. Let me tell you—when your season of elevation surfaces, one of the signs of this will be a greater degree of indifference and insecurity towards you. But I promise you, it's going to be okay!

Prophets let's get back to you really quickly here. I really want you to understand that as a prophet, you have the ability to touch what I call the "Prophetic Tier Three." You have the *ability* to stir up the spirit of prophecy and move in it. You have the *ability* to operate in the gift of prophecy. And finally, you have the *ability* to operate in the office of the prophet. The other two administrations can prophesy with a *certain degree* of prophetic grace…while the prophet has the governing authority to tap into *unlimited levels* of prophetic grace.

Power Point 53

The Core of the Prophetic Ministry

"The essence or the core of the prophetic ministry is not produced or confirmed by echoes and accolades of man— it is originated from the Holy Spirit."

"It is well and good when our convictions are based upon the *thou shalts* and the *thou shalt nots* of Scripture rather than our own ideas." ~Billy Graham

Core denotes a central and often foundational part, usually distinct from the enveloping part by a difference in nature.

It is so impossible to have an understanding of what I want to call the Code of Prophetic Ethics. There is a reality that we must function in a prophetic ministry gift. I strongly believe that somewhere along the way, we have forgotten this.

Cores are established by morals, beliefs, and convictions. Things you like, places you go, and how you communicate—core values that were established by some of our forefathers have brought us to this place where we are. Generals and giants of faith that have paved the way for us.

This word **conviction** is just one of the words associated with the word *core*. It is one of those words that not just only shapes your core belief system, but also forms your view and perception of the world.

> "Decide to be a man of conviction. *"Conviction of what?"* you may ask. Have a conviction about the things God has called you. Have a conviction about the things you are supposed to accomplish in your lifetime. Have a conviction about the things that God has told you. Live by these convictions! Be prepared to give up anything so that you can fulfill your conviction." ~Dag Heward Mills

> "We live our thoughts and manifest them in our attitudes toward ourselves and others. We cannot live beyond our thoughts and convictions." ~Dr. Myles Monroe

We must also understand as prophetic ministry gifts that when it comes down to the prophetic ministry, there's no need to imitate or plagiarize someone else's prophetic words. For example, the word **echo**, which many of us are familiar with, know that echoes are *a repeating of that which was said by the original sources.*

Echoes carry no weight or substance on their own. Echoes need to have a launching pad to be given life. Another great illustration is that of a shadow, which does not exist on its own—it must have something to reflect from.

Unfortunately, in our prophetic communities, there are a lot of echoes and shadows who are operating in the gifts, but who lack character, which is what places them in a place to perform and produce in the prophetic ministry. Your prophetic gift may get you in the room, but your character is what will give you an audience for you to stay in the room.

> "Whatever I am today is a product of that conviction that victory through Christ is victory indeed. The rest is history." ~Prophet T.B. Joshua

Power Point 54

Filtering Your Prophetic Gift Through Love

"When ministering in the office of the prophet, it is important to filter your prophetic flow through the venue of love. This is how we must function."

Before you fall in love with the prophetic, you must fall in love with God! Otherwise, you must be cautious of what I call the **Triple A Club: A**gendas, **A**ngles, and **A**mbitions. These are traits that can sabotage your prophetic gifts and purpose. They can also take away from the substance, character, and purity of the prophetic.

Not everyone has the right **A**genda when it comes to the prophetic ministry. The basics or logistics are always good to know and refer to regularly. The agenda of the prophetic is to simply help you understand and confirm the heart and mind of God concerning His plans for your life and family.

Now when it comes to **A**ngles, be careful of those you let get close to you. Unless you have strong discernment or wise counsel around you, you can't tell what a person's angle is for wanting to prophesy, know, or connect to you. People have all kinds of reasons why they want to be prophetic or walk in the office of a prophet.

Proverbs 11:14 KJV

> *"Where no counsel is, the people fall: but in the multitude of counsellors there is safety."*

Angles can be very deceptive with the intent to destroy you. I strongly encourage you to know those who are around you.

1 Thessalonians 5:12 KJV

> *"And we beseech you, brethren, that you come to know those who labor among you, and are over you in the Lord and admonish you..."*

Lastly, there is **A**mbition. Not all ambition is good; but neither is it all bad. Let us focus for a moment on the negative aspect of ambition. I want to spend some time here because this is a very prevalent spirit that is operating in the prophetic ministry today. An Absalom spirit has really infected the prophetic gift to an extent, which also has affected the way some people view the prophetic anointing. This spirit has a more love for *self* than it does for *service*. So, what better way than to expound on this than the story of Absalom, the third son of King David?

2 Samuel 15:1-14 NIV

> *"In the course of time, Absalom provided himself with a chariot and horses and with fifty men to run ahead of him. He would get up early and stand by the side of the road leading to the city gate. Whenever anyone came with a complaint to be placed before the king for a decision, Absalom would call out to him, 'What town are you from?' He would answer, 'Your servant is from one of the tribes of Israel.' Then Absalom would say to him, 'Look, your claims are valid and proper, but there is no representative of the king to hear you.' And Absalom would add, 'If only I were appointed judge in the land! Then*

everyone who has a complaint or case could come to me and I would see that they receive justice.'

Also, whenever anyone approached him to bow down before him, Absalom would reach out his hand, take hold of him and kiss him. Absalom behaved in this way toward all the Israelites who came to the king asking for justice, and so he stole the hearts of the people of Israel.

At the end of four years, Absalom said to the king, 'Let me go to Hebron and fulfill a vow I made to the Lord. While your servant was living at Geshur in Aram, I made this vow: 'If the Lord takes me back to Jerusalem, I will worship the Lord in Hebron.'

The king said to him, 'Go in peace.' So, he went to Hebron.

Then Absalom sent secret messengers throughout the tribes of Israel to say, 'As soon as you hear the sound of the trumpets, then say, "Absalom is king in Hebron." Two hundred men from Jerusalem had accompanied Absalom. They had been invited as guests and went quite innocently, knowing nothing about the matter. While Absalom was offering sacrifices, he also sent for Ahithophel the Gilonite, David's counselor, to come from Giloh, his hometown. And so, the conspiracy gained strength, and Absalom's following kept on increasing.

A messenger came and told David, 'The hearts of the people of Israel are with Absalom.'

Then David said to all his officials who were with him in Jerusalem, 'Come! We must flee, or none of us will escape from Absalom. We must leave

> *immediately, or he will move quickly to overtake us and bring ruin on us and put the city to the sword.'"*
>
> *"Now in all Israel there was no one as handsome as Absalom, so highly praised; from the sole of his foot to the crown of his head there was no defect in him."*
> **(2 Samuel 14:25)**

Physically, Absalom was blessed. He was admired by all; everyone wanted to "be like Absalom." He had all the things people in those positions usually have when others look longingly at them with wonder and awe and wish they could switch places.

In addition to his good looks, Absalom was smart; a very clever, cunning, and crafty fellow. He was very good at persuasion and had a likeable personality and great charm (**2 Samuel 15:6**). He had authority, being the son of the king. He had material wealth.

So, what could possibly go wrong? Plenty! There was a sharp contrast between Absalom's physical beauty and his spiritual poverty. His blessings were not his downfall, but rather his lack of spirituality was. He did not have what it takes within, and it is what is within that the Lord considers most important (**1 Samuel 16:7**).

If you notice, there are so many traits that we see in prophetic ministry gifts today. They are articulate, charismatic, and appear to know how to communicate the Word to a degree. They can dress and look the part and have great people skills but are disconnected by a lack of intimacy with the Holy Spirit. It is a spirit that is in error so that if the prophets of God are not in the place they should be, this spirit may influence and infect their prophetic gift.

Some of the interesting things I've discovered about this spirit is that it will often speak subtle, sneaky, secret words into the ears of those who are disgruntled, discontent, and often disconnected from the vision, membership, tribe, or group. Those that are often used by a spirit of Absalom have an attitude of spiritual pride that is misdirected and mismanaged.

I see this so often in our apostolic/prophetic churches. It's almost like it's becoming the norm for some circles or sects. The need has increased to become more prominent and noticeable as opposed to blessing people with the prophetic gift.

Let's look at some more characteristics of the **Absalom spirit** that infect the prophetic ministry:

- The Absalom spirit is cloaked in religion, and even though they put on a show of being submitted to leadership, they are not submitted in their heart. This is most likely what happened when Absalom went before King David to plead his case (**2 Sam. 14:33**).
- The Absalom spirit moves among the people and distorts not only the teaching, but the decisions of the leadership. Progressively discrediting and tearing down leadership is the only way in which Absalom can justify his rebellion in the eyes of his potential followers (**2 Sam. 15:3**).
- Those used by the spirit of Absalom conspire to manipulate the innocent.
- Those used by the spirit of Absalom use their own ideas as criteria for judgment.
- Those used by the spirit of Absalom disrupt establishment and order in a place.
- Those used by the spirit of Absalom lose their loyalty and servanthood.
- Those used by the spirit of Absalom maneuver for recognition and the praise of men.
- Those used by the spirit of Absalom suggest a better way and steal the hearts of the people. This happens very often in the prophetic ministry.

A biblical definition of ***ambition*** is defined as:

"To be strongly desirous," "to strive earnestly," "to make it one's aim."

The Body of Christ is full of ambitious believers. There are those who are willing to do whatever it takes, often at the expense of someone else's efforts. There are actually prophetic ministry gifts that are very ambitious. They become under-the-radar opportunists, looking for a moment to enter in, and are often driven by a desire to succeed with an unbalanced perspective.

We are in a culture where many people are more in love with the idea or concept of the prophetic than they are with loving God. The prophetic was not designed to be a substitute for knowing God personally! The love of God is so much more than the spirit of prophecy; however, it makes such a difference when love is the motive and undercurrent. At some point, we have built a society of "prophetic junkies" and dependents. At the end of the day, no one wants you prophesying to them from a place of hurt, resentment, or disdain. You shouldn't even have the green light to proceed in prophesying to someone. If the real Holy Spirit is present, He'll encourage you to get it straight first!

As prophets, we can make a consistent impact on the Body of Christ as we flow from a revelation of love and not just a revelation of the prophetic. I believe, one of the greatest disappointments in the prophetic ministry is that ministry gifts often forgot how to love God's people. This may stem from arrogance or pride. Ultimately, it doesn't matter what you *say*; however, it matters what you *do*.

Genesis 1:11 KJV

> *"And God said, Let the earth bring forth grass, the herb yielding seed, and the fruit tree yielding fruit after his kind, whose seed is in itself, upon the earth: and it was so."*

Luke 6:43-45 NIV

> *"No good tree bears bad fruit, nor does a bad tree bear good fruit. Each tree is recognized by its own fruit. People do not pick figs from thorn bushes, or grapes from briers. A good man brings good things out of the good stored up in his heart, and an evil man brings evil things out of the evil stored up in his heart. For the mouth speaks what the heart is full of."*

Galatians 5:22 KJV

"But the fruit of the Spirit is love, joy, peace, longsuffering, gentleness, goodness, faith…"

In these three verses here, we see how important it is to understand how to develop a fruit. A lot of Christians believe that they can just get by; however, this is not truth. Whatever fruit you are will be revealed.

Prophets, let's remember to practice what we've seen our Mentor and our Master do in His three years or so of ministry. There's so much we can glean from here. Jesus displayed more in three years than what some prophetic gifts have displayed in thirty years.

Jeremiah 31:2-4 NIV

"This is what the Lord says: 'The people who survive the sword will find favor in the wilderness; I will come to give rest to Israel.' The Lord appeared to us in the past, saying: 'I have loved you with an everlasting love; I have drawn you with unfailing kindness. I will build you up again, and you, Virgin Israel, will be rebuilt. Again, you will take up your timbrels and go out to dance with the joyful.'"

"You can *always* give without loving, but you can *never* love without giving."

"Love is the doorway through which the human soul passes from selfishness to service."

Prophets, let's love people as He loves us, with no agendas or motives—just because!

1 John 4:16-19 KJV

"And we have known and believed the love that God hath to us. God is love; and he that dwelleth in love dwelleth in God, and God in him.

> *Herein is our love made perfect, that we may have boldness in the day of judgment: because as he is, so are we in this world.*
>
> *There is no fear in love; but perfect love casteth out fear: because fear hath torment. He that feareth is not made perfect in love.*
>
> *We love him, because he first loved us."*

1 Corinthians 13:1-8 KJV

> *"Though I speak with the tongues of men and of angels, and have not charity, I am become as sounding brass, or a tinkling cymbal.*
>
> *And though I have the gift of prophecy, and understand all mysteries, and all knowledge; and though I have all faith, so that I could remove mountains, and have not charity, I am nothing.*
>
> *And though I bestow all my goods to feed the poor, and though I give my body to be burned, and have not charity, it profiteth me nothing.*
>
> *Charity suffereth long, and is kind; charity envieth not; charity vaunteth not itself, is not puffed up,*
>
> *Doth not behave itself unseemly, seeketh not her own, is not easily provoked, thinketh no evil;*
>
> *Rejoiceth not in iniquity, but rejoiceth in the truth;*
>
> *Beareth all things, believeth all things, hopeth all things, endureth all things.*
>
> *Charity never faileth: but whether there be prophecies, they shall fail; whether there be tongues, they shall cease; whether there be knowledge, it shall vanish away."*

This letter that Apostle Paul penned is so climactic. It speaks volumes to those of us who are in the faith or in ministry. It depicts a very strong case when it comes to displaying love that is unconditional and not superficial. Love is the current that helps establish commitment and covenant. Paul made this very evident and clear in his message to the Corinthian Church.

Revelation in the prophetic alone will not suffice! There must be in addition to a foundation, the glue that holds it all together, which is **love**.

Power Point 55

Continue to Present Your Bodies as a Sacrifice

"As a prophetic ministry gift, always remember that your title is not as important as your position of worship. Continue to present your body and life as a living sacrifice. Prophets especially, we should always be attracted to the glory realm because it creates and assists in an atmosphere for God to move."

Romans 12:1-8 NIV

> *"Therefore, I urge you, brothers and sisters, in view of God's mercy, to offer your bodies as a living sacrifice, holy and pleasing to God—this is your true and proper worship. Do not conform to the pattern of this world, but be transformed by the renewing of your mind. Then you will be able to test and approve what God's will is—his good, pleasing, and perfect will. For by the grace given me I say to every one of you: Do not think of yourself more highly than you ought, but rather think of yourself with sober judgment, in accordance with the faith God has distributed to each of you. For just as each of us has one body with many members, and these members do not all have the same function, so in*

> *Christ we, though many, form one body, and each member belongs to all the others. We have different gifts, according to the grace given to each of us. If your gift is prophesying, then prophesy in accordance with your faith; if it is serving, then serve; if it is teaching, then teach; if it is to encourage, then give encouragement; if it is giving, then give generously; if it is to lead, do it diligently; if it is to show mercy, do it cheerfully."*

We are in such a world where people are driven and impressed by titles and positions. When in actuality, none of this impresses God. Your exterior doesn't get His attention; it's your interior—what's in your heart.

1 Samuel 16:7 KJV

> *"But the Lord said unto Samuel, 'Look not on his countenance, or on the height of his stature; because I have refused him: for the Lord seeth not as man seeth; for man looketh on the outward appearance, but the Lord looketh on the heart.'"*

Mark 8:36-37 KJV

> *"For what shall it profit a man, if he shall gain the whole world, and lose his own soul?*
>
> *Or what shall a man give in exchange for his soul?"*

Somehow in our prophetic culture, we have focused more on the commercial aspect of the prophetic ministry. Of course, we need to promote the prophetic; but when the emphasis is more on an office or title in ministry, we have lost the purpose and direction that the prophetic can take us to.

Think about commercials. They are created to get your attention; to get you to focus on something or someone in particular. If you're not cautious and alert, you can become distracted by something visual, which may be detrimental to your prophetic assignment.

The devil would love *nothing more* than to pull you off of your God-given assignment. He will use those closest to you, those around you, and even some of your enemies. As prophets, we have to be careful not to let the title of the prophet rule, dictate, or determine our lifestyle. Titles don't hold the authority or power but are simply the description of the individual in a specific office. The ability and authority or action is locked up inside of that individual. In other words, what you have been doing all this time doesn't take away from who you are because of a title.

I have learned over the years that the real test of the call in any office is if you can do this when people don't honor you or recognize you as "Prophet Jack Frost" or "Prophet Georgia Mack." Can you function without the title or do you need it to validate your significance in society?

Luke 22:25-27 KJV

> "And he said unto them, 'the kings of the Gentiles exercise lordship over them; and they that exercise authority upon them are called benefactors.
>
> But ye shall not be so: but he that is greatest among you, let him be as the younger; and he that is chief, as he that doth serve.
>
> For whether is greater, he that sitteth at meat, or he that serveth? is not he that sitteth at meat? but I am among you as he that serveth.'"

I want to charge you to stay in a place like Jesus. It didn't matter to him if you were black, white, green, or red. Jesus remained a servant, which to me is the greatest title and the one many often struggle to accept and walk in. I encourage you to please stay low, stay humble, stay open, and God will promote you. There are a lot of people that have titles that they claim; however, God didn't confirm or approve those titles.

Psalm 75:5-7 KJV

"Lift not up your horn on high: speak not with a stiff neck.

For promotion cometh neither from the east, nor from the west, nor from the south.

But God is the judge: he putteth down one, and setteth up another."

One of the most important things I want you to take away from the book in addition to developing your prophetic gift, is the fact that your gift is spiritual, not natural. You may ask, *what exactly is it again?*

A spiritual gift is a God-given talent or ability, given to select Christians by the Holy Spirit that allows them to do service in their lives to benefit the Church and perform its mission on earth. From scriptural passages, Christians understand spiritual gifts as *"abilities or skills that are divinely provided in individuals."* The purpose of the spiritual gifts is to build up, inspire, and support the Church.

"The prophetic ministry or the office of a prophet is a spiritual assignment that is carried out through a willing or selected natural vessel."

Every successful person in the Word as it relates to the prophetic that has conquered, mastered, or walked in their calling has done something above the norm. They were willing to step out of that familiar place. Remember this: *nothing great ever comes out of a comfort zone*. Go for it and stretch out, and let's build together!

"Prophets, you are not normal, because the God that speaks through you is not normal, but supernatural! Walk in your assignment unapologetically and in confidence!"

"**Prophets, when you walk in your Metron with confidence, you will always get the attention of the spirit of Jezebel and the spirit of Saul. I charge you to push, to persevere, to plow, and to prophesy!**"

Appendix

Prophetic Decrees and Declarations

I declare that this will be the season that the Lord will resuscitate the life and the voice of His prophets, and that out of their mouths will be released rhythms and rivers of the prophetic that the body has never encountered.

I decree and declare that the prophets now will move in a greater depth of demonstration.

I declare that revelation will stir the hearts of men as God's prophets release the Word of the Lord.

I declare that God will activate such a passion for His presence as His prophets continue to develop.

I declare that humility will be the bread that the prophet eats in this hour to increase their prophetic capacity.

I declare portals, gates, doors, and windows of the prophetic will be exposed to the Body of Christ.

I declare and decree apostolic alignment and sensitivity over every prophet right now, in Jesus' Name.

A Short Summary of the Prophets in the Bible and Their Significance

Four Major Prophets:

Isaiah - Written in sixty-six chapters. It concentrates mainly on speaking to Israel but provides prophetic utterances on Judah and many other foreign nations. It is sometimes termed as the "Messianic prophetic book" because of the detail given about Jesus. The most famous verse is **7:14**, *"The virgin will conceive a child! She will give birth to a son and will call him Immanuel"*

The Book of Isaiah is one of the longest and most important books in the Old Testament. It covers the life of Isaiah and what he said and did as prophet of God. It is sometimes called a miniature Bible because it has sixty-six chapters and two major divisions. The first division is the first thirty-nine chapters, just like the Old Testament has thirty-nine books. The first thirty-nine chapters emphasize God's judgment on immoral and idolatrous men. The second division is the last twenty-seven chapters, just like there are twenty-seven books in the New Testament. These last chapters teach us about the return of the Jews from Babylonian captivity, and it teaches about the grace of God through the promised Messiah concluding with the final judgment. These last chapters are similar to the New Testament in that they offer a message of hope through our redeemer, Jesus.

Jeremiah - Written in fifty-two chapters. This prophetic book is a pre-exilic and post-exilic book, meaning the events that took place was a record of what happened before they went into exile and whilst were exile, and it also looks at the future. One of the most well-known verses is **Jeremiah 29:11**, *"For I know the thoughts that I think toward you, says the Lord, thoughts of peace and not of evil, to give you a future and a hope."*

Ezekiel - Written in forty-eight chapters. Its focus is on Israel and Judah. The book gives the prophetic view of the future temple that many call the *new messianic temple*. It describes vividly angelic beings and also graphically illustrates Judah's sin in sexual language. The most famous verse has to be about the valley of dry bones in **37:1**, *"The hand of the Lord was on me, and he brought me out by the Spirit of the Lord and set me in the middle of a valley; it was full of bones"*

Daniel - Written in twelve chapters. The book covers the period of the nobles of Judah in captivity at Babylon. Plus, there are long sections that cover the eschatological topics that dovetails into the Book of Revelation. Not to forget that the story of the three Hebrew boys and the fire is in this book! The most famous verse is **11:32b**, *"... but the people that do know their God shall be strong, and do exploits."*

12 Minor Prophets:

Hosea - Written over fourteen chapters. The book depicts the apostasy of Israel by requiring the prophet to marry a prostitute called Gomer—one of the most peculiar occurrences in the Bible. The most well-known verse, even by unbelievers, is **4:6**, *"My people are destroyed for lack of knowledge."*

Joel - Written in three chapters. The book depicts the punishment to be levied on Judah as well as its restoration. It also foretells the end times. There are two famous verses in this book: one about the locusts that God sent to ravage the land, and the second is the one Peter used in **Acts Chapter 2**. It is **Joel 2:28**, *"And it shall come to pass* *afterward, that I will pour out my Spirit on all flesh; your sons and your daughters shall prophesy, your old men shall dream dreams."*

Amos - Written over nine chapters. This prophetic book speaks to various nations then to Judah, and finally to Israel. I love **9:15** where God says, *"I will plant you in your own land and no longer will you be pulled up."* However, the most popular verse is **3:3** which says, *"How can two walk together, except they be agreed?"*

Obadiah - A short book of twenty-one verses. The vision is about the punishment God will levy on Edom in response to its attitude during the sufferings endured by Judah. The most famous verse has to be **1:18**, *"And the house of Jacob shall be a fire, and the house of Joseph a flame, and the house of Esau for stubble, and they shall kindle in them, and devour them; and there shall not be any remaining of the house of Esau; for the Lord hath spoken it."*

Jonah - Written over four chapters. No matter who you are, you have heard of the man that was swallowed by a big fish. Jonah was told by God to deliver a damning message to the city of Nineveh with the hope of repentance and restoration. Jonah goes to the opposite direction and God sends a fish to go get him back! The most popular verse is **1:17**, which was even part quoted by our Lord Jesus: *"Now the Lord had prepared a great fish to swallow Jonah and Jonah was in the belly of the fish three days and three nights."*

Micah - Written over seven chapters. The book conveys the vision of the prophet concerning Samaria and Jerusalem meaning Israel and Judah. It emphasizes the reasons why retribution will come up on these countries and also foretells their deliverance. The most famous verse is **5:2**, which is a messianic one that says, *"But you, Bethlehem Ephrathah, though you are small among the clans of Judah, out of you will come for me one who will be ruler over Israel, whose origins are from of old, from ancient times."*

Nahum - Written over three chapters. I think it was David Pawson that says, "this is the book Jonah wished he wrote." After Jonah delivered his verdict on the city of Nineveh, they repented. But a few years down the line, they plunged back into sin again and this time there would be no repentance or forgiveness. The most popular verse is **1:9**: *"What do ye contrive against the Lord? He will make an utter end; affliction shall not rise up the second time."*

Habakkuk - Written over three chapters. The prophet suggests that God is beholding evil and doing nothing about it. He questions why the Children of God would suffer from the hands of foreign powers, but God's response keeps him quiet. The most popular verse is **3:17**: *"Though the fig tree does not bud and there are no grapes on the vines, though the olive crop fails and the fields produce no food, though there are no sheep in the pen and no cattle in the stalls, yet I will rejoice in the Lord, I will be joyful in God my Savior."*

Zephaniah - Written over three chapters, the prophet depicts how God will expose the hidden sins of the people of Judah. God is pictured as one that would take up a lamp and search out what his children have been up to. The most popular and amazing verse is **3:17**: *"The Lord your God is with you, the Mighty Warrior who saves. He will take great delight in you; in his love he will no longer rebuke you but will rejoice over you with singing."*

Haggai - Written over two chapters. This post-exilic book exposes the attitude of the children of Israel when they returned to the land. They were consumed with building their own houses instead of focusing on completing God house. God reprimands them and their repentance is evidence in the ensuing actions. The most popular verse is **1:9**: *"Ye looked for much, and, lo it came to little; and when ye brought it home, I did blow upon it. Why? saith the Lord of hosts. Because of mine house that is waste, and ye run every man unto his own house."*

Zechariah - Written over fourteen chapters, the book follows post-exilic events until the second coming of Jesus. It constantly flows between what is going on in heaven and on earth. This is one of the books that illustrate how Satan accuses us just as he accused Joshua the high priest. The most popular verse is **4:6**: *"This is the Word of the Lord to Zerubbabel: Not by might, nor by power, but by my Spirit, says the Lord of hosts."*

Malachi - Written over four chapters. This book gives us the picture of what the children of Israel did when they returned into the land. They failed to sacrifice to God, and their priests went astray too. God questions their motives and then provides an awesome promise if they would respond by giving their tithes and offerings. The most popular verse has to be **3:10**: *"Bring the whole tithe into the storehouse, that there may be food in my house. Test me in this," says the Lord Almighty, "and see if I will not throw."*

Scriptures on Prophesying in the Amplified Bible

Acts 2:17 AMPC

"'And it shall come to pass in the last days," God declares, 'that I will pour out of My Spirit upon all mankind, and your sons and your daughters shall prophesy [telling forth the divine counsels] and your young men shall see visions (divinely granted appearances), and your old men shall dream [divinely suggested] dreams.'"

Acts 2:18 AMPC

"Yes, and on My menservants also and on My maidservants in those days I will pour out of My Spirit, and they shall prophesy [telling forth the divine counsels and predicting future events pertaining especially to God's kingdom]."

Acts 19:6 AMPC

"And as Paul laid his hands upon them, the Holy Spirit came on them; and they spoke in [foreign, unknown] tongues (languages) and prophesied."

Romans 12:6 AMPC

"Having gifts (faculties, talents, qualities) that differ according to the grace given us, let us use them: [He

whose gift is] prophecy, [let him prophesy] according to the proportion of his faith..."

1 Corinthians 12:10 AMP

"To another the working of miracles, to another prophetic insight (the gift of interpreting the divine will and purpose); to another the ability to discern and distinguish between [the utterances of true] spirits [and false ones], to another various kinds of [unknown] tongues, to another the ability to interpret [such] tongues."

1 Corinthians 13:2 AMPC

"And if I have prophetic powers (the gift of interpreting the divine will and purpose), and understand all the secret truths and mysteries and possess all knowledge, and if I have [sufficient] faith so that I can remove mountains, but have not love (God's love in me) I am nothing (a useless nobody)."

1 Corinthians 13:8 AMPC

"Love never fails [never fades out or becomes obsolete or comes to an end]. As for prophecy (the gift of interpreting the divine will and purpose), it will be fulfilled and pass away; as for tongues, they will be destroyed and cease; as for knowledge, it will pass away [it will lose its value and be superseded by truth]."

1 Corinthians 13:9 AMPC

"For our knowledge is fragmentary (incomplete and imperfect), and our prophecy (our teaching) is fragmentary (incomplete and imperfect)."

1 Corinthians 14:1 AMPC

"Eagerly pursue and seek to acquire [this] love [make it your aim, your great quest]; and earnestly desire and cultivate the spiritual endowments (gifts), especially that you may prophesy (interpret the divine will and purpose in inspired preaching and teaching)."

1 Corinthians 14:3 AMP

"But [on the other hand], the one who prophesies [who interprets the divine will and purpose in inspired preaching and teaching] speaks to men for their upbuilding and constructive spiritual progress and encouragement and consolation."

1 Corinthians 14:22 AMP

"Thus [unknown] tongues are meant for a [supernatural] sign, not for believers but for unbelievers [on the point of believing], while prophecy (inspired preaching and teaching, interpreting the divine will and purpose) is not for unbelievers [on the point of believing] but for believers."

1 Corinthians 14:24 AMPC

"But if all prophesy [giving inspired testimony and interpreting the divine will and purpose] and an unbeliever or untaught outsider comes in, he is told of his sin and reproved and convicted and convinced by all, and his defects and needs are examined (estimated, determined) and he is called to account by all."

1 Corinthians 14:29 AMP

"So, let two or three prophets speak [those inspired to preach or teach], while the rest pay attention and weigh and discern what is said."

1 Corinthians 14:31 AMPC

"For in this way you can give testimony [prophesying and thus interpreting the divine will and purpose] one by one, so that all may be instructed, and all may be stimulated and encouraged..."

1 Corinthians 14:39 AMPC

"So [to conclude], my brethren, earnestly desire and set your hearts on prophesying (on being inspired to preach and teach and to interpret God's will and purpose), and do not forbid or hinder speaking in [unknown] tongues."

1 Timothy 4:14 AMPC

"Do not neglect the gift, which is in you, [that special inward endowment] which was directly imparted to you [by the Holy Spirit] by prophetic utterance when the elders laid their hands upon you [at your ordination]."

Revelation 19:10 AMPC

"Then I fell prostrate at his feet to worship (to pay divine honors) to him, but he [restrained me] and said, Refrain! [You must not do that!] I am [only] another servant with you and your brethren who have [accepted and hold] the testimony borne by Jesus. Worship God! For the substance (essence) of the truth revealed by Jesus is the spirit of all prophecy

[the vital breath, the inspiration of all inspired preaching and interpretation of the divine will and purpose, including both mine and yours]."

Distinct Characteristics of Prophets Using the Letter "I" in Influencers:

- Prophets are **intentional**.
- Prophets are **intimate** with the Father.
- Prophets are **intercessors**.
- Prophets are **infused** with the Word and Spirit of God.
- Prophets don't **ignore** sin and injustice.
- Prophets hold fast to the **image** of Jesus.
- Prophets help **illuminate** the house of God.
- Prophets will often **illustrate** things to convey a point.
- Prophets love to **immerse** themselves in the spirit of worship.
- Prophets **impart** the Spirit of Truth.
- Prophets **import** messages from the Lord.
- Prophets assist in **implementing** the plan of the Lord for your life.
- Prophets **impose** upon the spirit of darkness as they release the prophetic Word of the Lord.
- Prophets **impregnate** you with a seed of hope.
- Prophets don't have the mind to try and **impress** people.
- Prophets help **improve** the culture of the Church.
- Prophets are not **impulsive**, but sensitive to the heartbeat of God.
- Prophets **incite** in the place or region they are assigned.
- Prophets always make sure they **include** God in their prophetic delivery.
- Prophets **incorporate** discernment in the prophetic process.
- Prophets are wired to **incline** unto the Lord in prayer.
- Prophets are not **independent** of God.
- Prophets are capable of **irrigating** a religious spirit.

- Prophets have the backing of God as they speak an **injunction** against Jezebel.
- Prophets allow the Holy Spirit to **inscribe** His plans on their hearts.
- Prophets have the ability to **invert** disorder and confusion that's in your life.
- Prophets **invest** their time with becoming familiar with the Father.
- Prophets develop a very strong prophetic **intuition**.
- Prophets are world changers and **influencers**!

An ***Influencer*** is *"an individual who has the power to affect the decisions of others because of his/her authority, knowledge, position, or relationship with his/her audience."*

Scriptures on the Three Things Jesus Emphasized to His Disciples That Will Increase Your Prophetic Gift

(All Scriptures are from the KJV.)

Prayer:

1 Samuel 1:12

> "And it came to pass, as she continued **praying** before the LORD, that Eli marked her mouth."

1 Samuel 1:26

> "And she said, 'Oh my lord, as thy soul liveth, my lord, I am the woman that stood by thee here, **praying** unto the LORD.'"

1 Kings 8:54

> "And it was so, that when Solomon had made an end of praying all this **prayer** and supplication unto the Lord, he arose from before the altar of the Lord, from kneeling on his knees with his hands spread up to heaven."

2 Chronicles 7:1

"Now when Solomon had made an end of **praying**, the fire came down from heaven, and consumed the burnt offering and the sacrifices; and the glory of the Lord filled the house."

Daniel 6:11

"Then these men assembled, and found Daniel **praying** and making supplication before his God."

Daniel 9:20

"And whiles I was speaking, and **praying**, and confessing my sin and the sin of my people Israel, and presenting my supplication before the Lord my God for the holy mountain of my God;"

Mark 11:25

"And when ye stand **praying**, forgive, if ye have ought against any: that your Father also which is in heaven may forgive you your trespasses."

Luke 1:10

"And the whole multitude of the people were **praying** without at the time of incense."

Luke 3:21

"Now when all the people were baptized, it came to pass, that Jesus also being baptized, and **praying**, the heaven was opened…"

Luke 9:18

"And it came to pass, as he was alone **praying**, his disciples were with him: and he asked them, saying, 'Whom say the people that I am?'"

Luke 11:1

"And it came to pass, that, as he was **praying** in a certain place, when he ceased, one of his disciples said unto him, 'Lord, teach us to pray, as John also taught his disciples.'"

Acts 11:5

"I was in the city of Joppa **praying**: and in a trance I saw a vision, A certain vessel descend, as it had been a great sheet, let down from heaven by four corners; and it came even to me..."

Acts 12:12

"And when he had considered the thing, he came to the house of Mary the mother of John, whose surname was Mark; where many were gathered together **praying**."

1 Corinthians 11:4

"Every man **praying** or prophesying, having his head covered, dishonoureth his head."

2 Corinthians 8:4

"**Praying** us with much entreaty that we would receive the gift, and take upon us the fellowship of the ministering to the saints."

Ephesians 6:18

"***Praying*** *always with all prayer and supplication in the Spirit, and watching thereunto with all perseverance and supplication for all saints..."*

Colossians 1:3

*"We give thanks to God and the Father of our Lord Jesus Christ, **praying** always for you."*

Colossians 4:3

*"Withal **praying** also for us, that God would open unto us a door of utterance, to speak the mystery of Christ, for which I am also in bonds..."*

1 Thessalonians 3:10

*"Night and day **praying** exceedingly that we might see your face, and might perfect that which is lacking in your faith?"*

Jude 1:20

*"But ye, beloved, building up yourselves on your most holy faith, **praying** in the Holy Ghost..."*

Esther 4:3

"And in every province, whithersoever the king's commandment and his decree came, there was great mourning among the Jews, and fasting, and weeping, and wailing; and many lay in sackcloth and ashes."

Fasting:

Esther 9:31

> "To confirm these days of Purim in their times appointed, according as Mordecai the Jew and Esther the queen had enjoined them, and as they had decreed for themselves and for their seed, the matters of the **fastings** and their cry."

Psalm 35:13

> "But as for me, when they were sick, my clothing was sackcloth: I humbled my soul with **fasting**; and my prayer returned into mine own bosom."

Psalm 69:10

> "When I wept, and chastened my soul with **fasting**, that was to my reproach."

Psalm 109:24

> "My knees are weak through **fasting**; and my flesh faileth of fatness."

Jeremiah 36:6

> "Therefore go thou, and read in the roll, which thou hast written from my mouth, the words of the Lord in the ears of the people in the Lord's house upon the **fasting** day: and also thou shalt read them in the ears of all Judah that come out of their cities."

Daniel 6:18

> "Then the king went to his palace, and passed the night **fasting**: neither were instruments of music brought before him: and his sleep went from him."

Daniel 9:3

*"And I set my face unto the Lord God, to seek by prayer and supplications, with **fasting**, and sackcloth, and ashes…"*

Joel 2:12

*"Therefore, also now, saith the Lord, turn ye even to me with all your heart, and with **fasting**, and with weeping, and with mourning…"*

Matthew 15:32

*"Then Jesus called his disciples unto him, and said, I have compassion on the multitude, because they continue with me now three days, and have nothing to eat: and I will not send them away **fasting**, lest they faint in the way."*

Matthew 17:21

*"Howbeit this kind goeth not out but by prayer and **fasting**."*

Mark 8:3

*"And if I send them away **fasting** to their own houses, they will faint by the way: for divers of them came from far."*

Mark 9:29

*"And he said unto them, this kind can come forth by nothing, but by prayer and **fasting**."*

Luke 2:37

> "And she was a widow of about fourscore and four years, which departed not from the temple, but served God with **fastings** and prayers night and day."

Acts 10:30

> "And Cornelius said, 'Four days ago I was **fasting** until this hour; and at the ninth hour I prayed in my house, and, behold, a man stood before me in bright clothing...'"

Acts 14:23

> "And when they had ordained them elders in every church, and had prayed with **fasting**, they commended them to the Lord, on whom they believed."

Acts 27:33

> "And while the day was coming on, Paul besought them all to take meat, saying, this day is the fourteenth day that ye have tarried and continued **fasting**, having taken nothing."

Giving:

Romans 4:20

> "He staggered not at the promise of God through unbelief; but was strong in faith, **giving** glory to God..."

1 Corinthians 14:7

*"And even things without life **giving** sound, whether pipe or harp, except they give a distinction in the sounds, how shall it be known what is piped or harped?"*

1 Corinthians 14:16

*"Else when thou shalt bless with the spirit, how shall he that occupieth the room of the unlearned say Amen at thy **giving** of thanks, seeing he understandeth not what thou sayest?"*

2 Corinthians 6:3

*"**Giving** no offence in any thing, that the ministry be not blamed…"*

Ephesians 5:4

*"Neither filthiness, nor foolish talking, nor jesting, which are not convenient: but rather **giving** of thanks."*

Ephesians 5:20

*"**Giving** thanks always for all things unto God and the Father in the name of our Lord Jesus Christ…"*

Philippians 4:15

*"Now ye Philippians know also, that in the beginning of the gospel, when I departed from Macedonia, no church communicated with me as concerning **giving** and receiving, but ye only."*

Colossians 1:12

*"**Giving** thanks unto the Father, which hath made us meet to be partakers of the inheritance of the saints in light…"*

Colossians 3:17

*"And whatsoever ye do in word or deed, do all in the name of the Lord Jesus, **giving** thanks to God and the Father by him."*

1 Timothy 2:1

*"I exhort therefore, that, first of all, supplications, prayers, intercessions, and **giving** of thanks, be made for all men…"*

Scriptures on Gifts and How to Use Them

(All Scriptures are from the KJV.)

Proverbs 18:16

*"A man's **gift** maketh room for him, and bringeth him before great men."*

Matthew 5:14-16

"Ye are the light of the world. A city that is set on an hill cannot be hid.

Neither do men light a candle, and put it under a bushel, but on a candlestick; and it giveth light unto all that are in the house.

Let your light so shine before men, that they may see your good works, and glorify your Father which is in heaven."

Romans 11:29

*"For the **gifts** and calling of God are without repentance."*

Romans 12:6-8

*"Having then **gifts** differing according to the grace that is given to us, whether prophecy, let us prophesy according to the proportion of faith;*

Or ministry, let us wait on our ministering: or he that teacheth, on teaching;

Or he that exhorteth, on exhortation: he that giveth, let him do it with simplicity; he that ruleth, with diligence; he that sheweth mercy, with cheerfulness."

1 Corinthians 10:31

"Whether therefore ye eat, or drink, or whatsoever ye do, do all to the glory of God."

1 Corinthians 12:4-6

*"Now there are diversities of **gifts**, but the same Spirit.*

And there are differences of administrations, but the same Lord.

And there are diversities of operations, but it is the same God which worketh all in all."

1 Corinthians 13:2 KJV

*"And though I have the **gift** of prophecy, and understand all mysteries, and all knowledge; and though I have all faith, so that I could remove mountains, and have not charity, I am nothing."*

Ephesians 2:10

*"Every good **gift** and every perfect gift is from above, and cometh down from the Father of lights,*

with whom is no variableness, neither shadow of turning."

Ephesians 4:7-8

"But unto every one of us is given grace according to the measure of the gift of Christ.

Wherefore he saith, when he ascended up on high, he led captivity captive, and gave **gifts** unto men."

Colossians 3:23-24

"And whatsoever ye do, do it heartily, as to the Lord, and not unto men;

Knowing that of the Lord ye shall receive the reward of the inheritance: for ye serve the Lord Christ."

Hebrews 2:4

"God also bearing them witness, both with signs and wonders, and with divers miracles, and **gifts** of the Holy Ghost, according to his own will?"

James 1:17

"Every good **gift** and every perfect gift is from above, and cometh down from the Father of lights, with whom is no variableness, neither shadow of turning."

2 Timothy 1:6

"Wherefore I put thee in remembrance that thou stir up the **gift** of God, which is in thee by the putting on of my hands."

1 Peter 4:10-11 KJV

*"As every man hath received the **gift**, even so minister the same one to another, as good stewards of the manifold grace of God.*

If any man speak, let him speak as the oracles of God; if any man minister, let him do it as of the ability which God giveth: that God in all things may be glorified through Jesus Christ, to whom be praise and dominion for ever and ever. Amen."

Prayer for Prophetic Ministry Gifts

Lord, I come to you now asking for forgiveness, if in any way I've pushed back, drawn back, or walked away.
I acknowledge Jesus as my Lord and Savior.
I realize, He is the best thing that has ever happened to me.
Lord, I ask for Your continued guidance and direction as I function in the prophetic anointing.
I want to be an example that honors You and makes You proud.
Show me how to love Your people, even when I'm struggling to love them.
Create in me a pure passion and heart for the prophetic;
I cannot do this without You, God.
There's so much going on in my world, and I need to stay focused on You, Lord.
So, I cast my thoughts and cares on You.
You said to trust in You and lean not to my own understanding,
You said that we should always pray and not faint,
You said to those that wait on You, that You'd increase their strength,
You said if we confess our sins that You're faithful to forgive us.
So, Lord I lay myself at your feet,

I lay my flesh down,
I lay my will down,
I lay my life down.
There's no other place for me to go other than to come to You.
I love You, Lord, with all my heart.
Please me help me to see right.
Help me to operate in prophetic integrity.
Help me to operate in purity.
Help me to understand the real reason why I prophesy.
I surrender my prophetic gift under Your accountability.,
God, cause my discernment to kick in like never before.
Lord, give me back my passion to pray more.
To study Your Word more and to fast more.
Any negative spirits that may have influenced my gift,
Whether by social media, family, or friends,
I renounce them now and take authority—
I take it back over my mind, in Jesus' Name.
And, Father, I thank You that You are sending people into my life to help cultivate the prophetic gift in me.
Father, I thank You for sending the right mentors and teachers in my life.
Thank you, Father, for planting me and keeping me rooted and grounded in a set house.
God, I thank You that this will be the year that I walk in my Metron, unapologetically and with boldness, in Jesus' Name.

Prophecy

"No Carryovers and Miscarriages in the next Crossover… only Full Term!
"You shall not carry over in this next crossover," says the Lord.

*"Lack **shall not cross over**…sickness **shall not cross over**…depression **shall not cross over**…bloodline curses **shall not cross over**, and the internal oppressor that has held you stagnant **shall not cross over** this time; for the hard place…even the very difficult place…will I address, make smooth and plane."* says the Lord.

"For many of you who felt the pressure of your past, and even your present, know this; I am releasing the breaker before you." **(Micah 2:13)**

*"Now go again. I say, **go again**! And this time it will be different. I have called you, My sons and daughters, to rise and conquer; the shift is imminent and the portals of prosperity and repositioning are about to open wide over your heads,"* says the Lord.

"That which has held you down and held you back is about to break in you and around you, for I am ending the hold!

*For even as blind Bartimaeus begin to cry even louder, **so shall you**.*

Raise up a shout in your city! Raise up a shout in your church! Witness the coming down of my glory!

Your season of imprisonment mentally and physically is over, and your season of empowerment is here," says the Lord.

"For many of you that have miscarried in the spirit, and even in the natural, know that I am shutting the doors of delay and in this season you will you experience full term; many unexpected pregnancies, both natural and spiritual, will occur for those who couldn't see before you," says the Lord.

"In your ministry and assignments. In your place of business and even your family," says the Lord .

"For I, the Lord, have been birthing something major and massive in you that will start a new trend for your life."

I hear the Lord saying , "1-2-3, push. 1-2-3, push. 1-2-3, push.

Push, My daughters; and push, My sons. Know this. I have established for you a delivery date. Get ready, for the year 2020 will birth and release many unexpected and unexplainable miracles," says the Lord.

"I prophesy that a surge has just been sent to your address and it has the supernatural written all over it.

No more carryovers and leftovers in 2020.

New; new; new; and that which you've haven't seen before.

Properties, business deals, settlements, and supernatural inheritances," says the Lord.

"I've been waiting to bless. I've been waiting to promote. I've been waiting to increase you," says the Lord.

"Your days of not having the strength to produce and birth are over; I'm releasing my midwives in the spirit." **(Isaiah 37:3)**

*"Your season of full term is here. It's here **now**. Receive it and claim it!"*

(Ezekiel 12:21-25 NIV)

"The word of the Lord came to me: 'Son of man, what is this proverb you have in the land of Israel: 'The days go by and every vision comes to nothing?' Say to them, "This is what the Sovereign Lord says: 'I am going to put an end to this proverb, and they will no longer quote it in Israel.'" Say to them, 'The days are near when every vision will be fulfilled. For there will be no more false visions or flattering divinations among the people of Israel. But I the Lord will speak what I will, and it shall be fulfilled without delay. For in your days, you rebellious people, I will fulfill whatever I say,' declares the Sovereign Lord."

Recommended Resources for Reading

Prophets, Pitfalls and Principles: God's Prophetic People Today by Bill Hamon

Prophets and the Prophetic Movement: God's Prophetic Move Today by Bill Hamon

The Prophets Dictionary: The Ultimate Guide to Supernatural Wisdom by Dr. Paula A. Price

Basic Training for the Prophetic Ministry by Kris Vallotton

Prophetic Ministry by Ron McKenzie

Practical Prophetic Ministry: The Metamorphosis of the Prophet by Colette Toach

You Can All Prophesy: A Balanced Approach to Giving and Receiving Personal Prophecy by Dennis Cramer

God Secrets: A Life Filled with Words of Knowledge by Shawn Bolz

The Making of a Prophet: Practical Advice for Developing Your Prophetic Voice by Jennifer LeClaire

The Prophetic Mantle: The Gift of Prophecy and Prophetic Operations in the Church Today by Roderick L. Evans

The Prophets Manual: A Guide to Sustaining your Prophetic Gift by John Eckhardt

The Seer: The Prophetic Power of Visions, Dreams and Open Heavens by James Goll

The Discerner: Hearing, Confirming, and Acting on Prophetic Revelation by James Goll

Growing in the Prophetic: A practical biblical guide to dreams, visions, and spiritual gifts by Mike Bickle

God Still Speaks: How to Hear and Receive Revelation from God for Your Family, Church, and Community by John Eckhardt

Increasing Your Prophetic Gift: Developing a Pure Prophetic Flow by Bill Vincent

Author Biography

"Many call him **'The Mail Man'** because of his on-point delivery of the Word of God. To others, he's an anointed vessel with a "right now" word for a prepared people..."

Dr. D. John Coleman is declaring the Word of the Lord in a time in which he has labeled "the changing of the guards." He was called by God at the age of seventeen and was licensed and ordained at the age of nineteen under the Pentecostal Assemblies of the World (P.A.W.). Dr. John has:

an AA Degree in Business Management from Phillips College

a Bachelor of Arts in Ministry with an Emphasis on Biblical Studies

a Master of Arts in Christian Education

a Doctor of Philosophy in Ministry from Midwest Christian College and Seminary

Dr. John has a mandate to bring a realization to the Body of Christ that it is God's desire for His people to establish a *relationship* with Him, instead of a "religion-ship." He is playing a pivotal part in reaching this generation and equipping them to activate the gifts within them. A cloud of testimonies including financial and healing miracles have manifested as a result of his ministry.

He has authored five previous books:

- *Power Points to Prosperous Living*
- *The Chambers of Chenaniah – 12 Foundational Truths to Praise & Worship*
- *Spiritual Reflections – 52 Prophetic Tips to Prevent Prophetic Slips*
- *Worship Wisdom 4:24 – Reset My Worship*
- *Rising of the Thoroughbreds – A Guide to Finding Balance in Prophetic Ministry*

One point that he emphasizes in one of his books is:

"There are two types of people that come in your life: those that *inspire* you and those that *expire* you."

Along with his wife, Dr. John has spearheaded many community initiatives and outreach programs, raising tens of thousands of dollars to help families in need. Their effect and contributions in the communities that they service are too numerous to mention. He has traveled and preached locally, nationally, and internationally, yet he is committed to his family and church, Kingdom Church International, a non-denominational assembly which he co-founded with his wife, where he is the apostolic overseer. Their vision for the church, which has a presence in Chicago and the south suburbs, is to "Empower God's People for Kingdom Living and Kingdom Advancement in the Earth."

Dr. John and his wife, Kisia, live in a suburb of Chicago and are the proud parents of five children: two boys and three girls; which include his orphaned nephew and two nieces.

Author Contact Information

Subscribe to our YouTube @ D. John Coleman Ministries

Facebook @ Deland John Coleman or

Prophet D. John Coleman

Twitter @ Delandjcoleman

Instagram @ d.johncoleman2020

For bookings, contact info@trykci.org.

www.ingramcontent.com/pod-product-compliance
Lightning Source LLC
Chambersburg PA
CBHW071337080526
44587CB00017B/2873